Sarah's Story

Lillian
Cantleberry

Publishing House
St. Louis

Copyright © 1983 Concordia Publishing House
3558 S. Jefferson Avenue, St. Louis, MO 63118
Manufactured in the United States of America.

Library of Congress Cataloging in Publication Data

Cantleberry, Lillian, 1922-
      Sarah's story.

      Includes index.
      1. Sarah (Biblical character)—Fiction. 2. Abraham (Biblical patriarch)—Fiction. I. Title.
PS3553.A547S3 1983   813'.54   82-25254
ISBN 0-570-03898-7 (pbk.)

   2 3 4 5 6 7 8 9 10   DB   92 91 90 89 88 87 86

Contents

Part One

Called Out

1

This is what the Lord, the God of Israel, says: "Long ago your forefathers, including Terah the father of Abraham and Nahor, lived beyond the River and worshiped other gods."   *Joshua 24:2*

I was called by two names—Sarai, meaning "like a princess," and Sarah, meaning "princess."

When I was young, had the best the world could offer, was aware of no lack of any kind in my life, I had the lesser name of Sarai. When I was old, locked into a way of life the world looked down on, and realized my inconsistencies and needs, God renamed me Sarah!

I lived in the most wondrous city in the world, married well, and took for granted our family would become a ruling power in the great Ur of the Chaldees. Abram and I had gigantic plans for his place in our contemporary society. He would be an integral part of the government, molding the growth of Ur as it increased in prestige, power and wealth. And I would be at his side.

The meaning of my name encouraged me to be of this mind, and Abram and I truly believed his name, meaning "exalted father," was prophetic. We had not the slightest doubt that we soon would live out our grand imaginings of how things should be.

And we would have many fine sons who would follow us, ruling wisely in Ur—and they would have sons who would do the same. Ours would be a lasting dynasty in this glorious land of the Chaldeans!

I can close my eyes and let my mind see the places I knew so well. Hard-packed earth streets absorbed the warmth of the Sumerian sun and, like brown ribbons, tied the city together. Canals reflected the sun and made the city sparkle.

At the center of Ur was the market place. My maid-servants and I shopped there many times for both the necessities and luxuries. There were market stalls for fruit, cheese, olives, dates, flour, and meat. Artisans sold their fine rugs, ornamental pieces of wood and ivory and shell, elegantly carved furniture, costly fabrics.

Along the outlying streets there was a great array of public buildings, palaces, mansions, and smaller houses. Bordering the city were very large estates. We lived on one of these estates and our compound was like a self-contained village.

But the dominant structure in Ur was the temple to the moon god, Nannar, with the altar for his goddess wife, Nin-Gal, close beside. The temple area occupied a large city block. Many cities and villages had natural "high places" for their temples and altars, but in the flat terrain of Ur our "high place" which rose 70 feet above the street had to be man-made. It took millions of bricks for the structure—bricks made from the river clay and bonded together with slime from the bitumen pits. Its finished splendor never suggested such common things as bricks and slime.

Our ziggurat was a rectangular, three-storied structure. Each level sat back from the one beneath it so it had a pyramidlike shape. At the top was the shrine of silver and blue enamel. It glistened, jewel-bright, and drew the eyes of people to it in wonder at its perfection. To most who looked at it, it was magnificent. To me it became a foreboding reminder of the abominable high point of the moon god worship. It happened on the first day of the new year—in the spring.

Abram and I were part of the crowd walking toward the temple area. He had attended the celebration before, but I had not. As we walked, he tried to explain to me the meaning of all the things which were going on, but it was difficult to hear him. The city was filled with competing sounds of ram's horns, cymbals, pipes, tambourines, lyres, and drums as processions of musicians marched around and around the base of the tower. A pair of wrestlers, portraying the gods Gilgamesh and his rival Enkidu, were locked in combat on an oval platform at the base of the tower, and onlookers were shouting encouragements to the favorite god. Girls dressed in brightly colored costumes were performing ceremonial dances. Priests were chanting. Pilgrims and townspeople, pressing in on the central site, engaged in animated conversations. Added to this were the sounds— and smells—of the numberless animals brought for temple sacrifice.

The gold idol of Nannar, five times as large as a man, was paraded by the priests through the streets. It bore the traditional symbols of authority—a ring and the tools of an architect. Many of the moon god worshipers followed the retinue of priests who carried the dazzling statue through the city streets, finally returning to the temple area and to the steps leading to the shrine.

A throne had been set up on the second level of the ziggurat. By the throne stood a grotesquely masked man, dressed like royalty in a richly fringed, embroidered ankle-length tunic which hung in vertical folds. The priest motioned for him to be seated on the throne, and at once he was besieged with mock homage shouted by the people. He was a prisoner from a recent war with a neighboring city-state, and he had been selected to be the new year's king for a day. At the end of the day he would be hanged from a noose which was already being put in place on an extension from the ziggurat wall.

Abram and I were more like observers than participants. I felt a sickening uneasiness as I saw that noose. Surely they would not...I could not frame the words, even in my mind...surely they would not...!

The splendor of the temple area, the excitement of the milling crowds, the magnetism of the music and the chanting, the cries of homage to the "king"—all combined to cram the eyes, ears, and minds of the people with an escalated frenzy of celebration that was intoxicating. And this highly charged atmosphere became even more dreadfully overpowering! The statue of Nannar had been carried slowly up to its shrine by the priests. It now towered over a beautiful young priestess who had been escorted up the steps by two priests. She was the one chosen to become Nannar's bride.

I had marvelled at the dignity of the young woman as she ascended to the waiting altar and, as if hypnotized, I leaned forward, squinting in order to see more clearly. The drums were at their loudest now. The other assorted noises were mounting in a maddening crescendo.

As the priests bound her to the altar, she struggled briefly. One slender arm, covered with jeweled bracelets, shot momentarily into the air. The myriads of gems adorning that arm reflected the far away sun and the ready torch!

I reached for Abram's steadying arm. I became quite ill, and he hurried me home.

From my bedroom window I could see the temple in the distance. For all its renown and grandeur it had become a monstrosity to me. I loosened the golden chains holding dark purple draperies at my windows so the view was blotted out. But my mind still could see it.

For the next several days Abram and I stayed in our home. All business was suspended in Ur because the city would be caught up in days and nights of dancing and debauchery. You could not walk in Ur without seeing the temple. You could not live in Ur and not be under its dominance.

Abram and I had taken minimal part in the routine

worship of Nannar and Nin-Gal through the years, but I had been experiencing less and less of any emotion akin to worship, even before the new year debacle. I was bothered by increasing doubts and resentments toward the gods. My scant homage to them was because of a lingering, fearful superstition about them. I had kept these negative thoughts to myself, but now, with the memory of the "king for a day" and the "bridal ceremony" overwhelming me, I could no longer keep still. The day after that new year celebration I ran to Abram with a barrage of hysterical questions.

"What value is a dead girl to a golden god? What is the need for that 'king for a day' to be killed? Who decides what sacrifices a silent god desires?"

As soon as I had voiced the questions I felt free of an enormous emotional burden, but guilty of a mortal sin for having spoken so against the gods.

Abram had a special way of looking when he was evading an issue. It involved a lifted chin, head tossed slightly to one side, half a smile and a shrug of the shoulders. He looked this way as he tried to find some profound words to deal with my heresy. Then he simply said, "I do not question the priests, the wise ones who understand the gods. Nor should you."

His tone of voice indicated our discussion, brief and inadequate as it was, had come to an end. But the subject was still very much in my mind and I knew it was still in Abram's mind because he, like I, did not like unanswered questions. I knew we both doubted the priests and the gods more than we openly acknowledged. Our minds were battlegrounds of frustrations, for we vaguely knew of another God who was not like these deities of Ur.

Abram spoke occasionally of this other God. Father Terah, grandfather Nahor, and their ancestors before them knew of Him. Each passed this knowledge down to the next generation.

Abram's evasive answer to my unthinkable questions

gave me no indication of how intently he, too, had been considering the inadequacy and absurdity of Ur's gods. He told me later that for many months before the day I confronted him with my own feelings he had been experiencing an inner withdrawal from them. That gradual detachment opened the way for increased objectivity about them—and revulsion of them! At the same time he was being pulled away from Ur's deities, he was being filled with a longing to know more about the God of his fathers.

Even so, for more than a year after our short theological discussion, we resumed our daily routine and generally found life pleasant and easy in our city. We stifled our doubts about its religious practices and routinely discharged the ceremonial obligations required. We stayed away from the next new year's celebration, but, aware of what was going on, we relived the previous year's haunting scenes in our mind.

For the most part, our days were busy and productive. Our large living quarters in the spacious home of Terah required a lot of overseeing. I was occupied with the details of a well-run household, directing servants in work to be done each day, purchases to be made, guest rooms to be made ready, special menues to be served, and sewing projects to be done. Life was exciting, and the time passed quickly, merging weeks into months.

Abram went daily to his place of work at the main city gate. He supervised collecting taxes on caravans headed to and from Babylon, Damascus, and the remote cities of Egypt. He learned much from the travelers about life along, and beyond, the Euphrates River. I enjoyed having him in this work because the caravaneers usually gave him beautiful pieces of art work—tapestries, thick rugs, gold and silver bowls, and sometimes jewelry or perfume.

Day followed day with fairly predictable events.

But emotional lightning was about to destroy any complacency!

2

But I took your father Abraham from the land beyond the River . . . .
Joshua 24:3

*I*t was early afternoon, much too early for Abram
to come home. But he rushed through the door from the
house, calling as he hurried to the place in the garden where
he knew I would be.

"Sarai!" He was nearly breathless.

"Abram! What is it?"

"We are moving!"

"Moving? From the loveliest house in Ur? Why?"

"We are moving, but not to any other house in this city.
We are leaving Ur!"

"Leaving Ur?" I parroted his last two words but my tone
of voice was quite different from the one he had used. I said
it again, as if in shock, as if by hearing my own voice say it, I
might believe what I had just heard. "Leave Ur?"

Neither of us spoke for the next few moments. I could
feel my heart pounding hard and knew my face was turning
an unbecoming shade of red! I waited for him to speak,
hoping he would tell me he had been teasing and I should
forget all about it.

In the strained silence I groped for some reasons for this
bizarre situation. I groped for reason itself! Then, in a
strangely subdued voice I asked, "Abram, what are you
saying? What do you mean?"

"I am saying, and I mean—we are moving."

"Where? Where are we moving? What place could

compare to Ur? Our family and friends are here. Our home is here. Your work is here. Everything is here!"

"No, Sarai!" Now Abram was shouting, "Not everything is here!"

"Everything I want is here! And you didn't tell me yet where we are moving, and why the move is necessary. Tell me!" By this point I was screaming, ignoring his hand raised in quiet authority to signal me to stop the tirade. I screamed even louder, "Where are we moving? How soon do we have to move? Why are we moving?"

Abram's stronger voice could surge over mine any time he chose to have it do so, as at that moment. "Sarai, you talk so fast! You ask the same questions twice. You don't give me time to answer between the questions. Be still!"

It would have been grand if I had said something serene like, "Of course, Abram. I will move wherever you want. Now tell me, please, what this is all about."

But I didn't say that. It would have been so unnatural that even now it makes me smile. It would have put Abram in as deep a shock as I was in at the time. I could have handled it all much better than I did, but self-control was drowned in the burst of emotions that surfaced at Abram's unbelievable statements. I was temporarily without much common sense or even my customary courtesy.

Perhaps he could have been more tactful in telling me this tremendous piece of news. If only he could have told me what had preceded it — his unique experience. He couldn't, and even if he had told me, I would not have believed him.

We stood looking at each other, each seeing a stranger. I did not understand what seemed to be his selfish, high-handed, life-changing decision. He did not understand my defensive adoration of my house and the things in it — of my city and the ones there whom I loved.

At least I obeyed his last words to me. I was being quiet. I bit my lip to be quiet. I raised my eyes to the sky and tried to breathe deeply to be quiet.

Into this quietness came the familiar voice of my husband—but his words were unimaginable. If I had been shocked by his initial announcement about moving, I was dazed by his amplification of it! I never could remember the actual words he used but their meaning was clear, causing my heart to pound faster and my face to grow even more red. He didn't have to tell me to be still now. I could think of no words to use in reply, and I had no strength to voice them if I could think of any. Numbly I went over them in my mind.

Yes, we would move. Yes, it would be soon. He didn't know what the destination would be. We would live in tents.

NO! All I could think of was, "NO!"

A tent! Regression! Inconvenience! Hardship! No family near! No social life! Boredom! Futility! Ridiculous absurdity!

I was swamped with unbelief, confusion and anger—all at the same time. Further talk would have been useless. First I must get control of my emotions, and quickly!

Deliberately, I took my mind away from this incomprehensible encounter, determined to concentrate possessively and calmly on the house I was to give up—for a tent!

Even now, so many years later, when that house has long since ceased to be my treasured possession, I can recall its wondrous detail.

It was built in the design of a sprawling square. Entry was made through intricately carved double doors of cedar wood. Two stories of spacious rooms were built in each corner of the square, connected by covered walkways on the ground level and by a wooden balcony on the second story.

In the center, enclosed by the great house, was our garden. Flowers were planted in precise color patterns. Shrubs were carefully trimmed. There were small trees which bore sweet blossoms and fruit. A mosaic walkway led through the garden, passing several marble benches and a latticed garden house, and encircling our crescent-shaped pool. The pool reflected its border of red, yellow and blue flowers during the day, and by night it reflected the warm light from the lamps placed around it and the cool light from the stars and the moon. We spent much time in the garden. It had a special beauty by day and by night, with fragrances as fascinating as its design and color.

On the lower level of the house there were no windows on the outer side, but there were large windows looking out on our garden. Upstairs there were windows on both sides, covered by delicate latticework, so we could see out but have complete privacy.

Our apartment was on the northeast side. Terah's rooms and business quarters occupied the southeast apartment. He shared his rooms with his grandson, Lot, who had made his home in Ur following the death of his father, Haran, some months before. The southwest corner was furnished for house guests. The northwest corner was the great hall — its ceiling two stories high with balconies on three sides. Abram liked nothing more than to have house guests and to entertain them lavishly at banquets in the great hall.

A wide expanse of land lay between our house and the road from the city. As protection from high winds that swept across this area, lovely orchards and rows of taller trees had been planted. Adjacent to the groves of trees were the vegetable gardens, the servants' quarters, the workshops, and the stables. Terah had set aside several acres for open fields where he could conduct military drills with his servants who also served as the guards of his estate. Guards were needed even though our land was encircled by a high wall. Tereh's wealth was a matter of common knowledge around Ur, and there had been serious attempts to rob and vandalize.

Our house was just about perfect. Abram and I entertained our friends often, partly because we enjoyed their company—but also because we liked to show off our lovely home.

Reality suddenly broke in on my effort to think of something pleasant.

A tent! A tent! The transitory truce between Abram and me was about to be ended. I ventured one more question.

"How long are we to live in a tent?"

"I don't know. We are to pack up and start out alone—with a minimum number of servants, some flocks of sheep and goats, and basic household items. Most of our things can be given to our family and friends. We will not need to take much with us."

"Give our things away?" My voice sounded as unreal to me as the words I said. Surely, surely I was dreaming. If not, could Abram be dreaming?

We talked on for a while without any real communication. A feeling of helplessness engulfed me. Then we both became quiet and the silence was as a high wall between us.

_____*3*

The Lord had said to Abram, "Leave your country, your people and your father's household . . . ."   *Genesis 12:1*

*L*ater that evening, after a supper neither of us wanted, we walked outdoors and sat on a garden bench. Abram began to speak, but abruptly stopped. He got up impatiently from the bench and walked several long strides away. He stood motionless except for absentmindedly clenching and unclenching his right fist. He was looking toward the star-crowded heavens as though he expected to hear a voice or see a vision. He was intensely alert.

I had no desire to reopen a conversation that would cause either of us any further anxiety. I hoped that, given enough time and neglect, the whole trauma of the afternoon would fade away, and we could get on with our everyday work and plans and delights.

I thought perhaps Abram had been working too hard at his job. Father Terah was getting quite old, and this was a worry to him. There had been some difference of opinion with his brother, Nahor, resulting in Nahor's moving his family to the city of Haran, where Terah had lived years ago. Also, Abram was getting anxious—as I was—because we had no sons yet. That was it! An accumulation of depressing things had discouraged him, and he had indulged in a childish fantasy of wanting to run away from everything and everyone.

But he had said "we" were moving—at least he did not want to run away from me! That kind of thinking cooled my smoldering temper a bit. Whatever else he wanted to leave, whoever else he never wanted to see again, he did want me with him! He did love me. And oh, did I love him! As greatly as I wanted more and more of Ur's luxuries and its sophisticated people, to have all that without Abram would have been to have nothing. The brief thought of me without my beloved brought instant tears, and I felt a choking weight in my throat which blocked the words I wanted to say to him.

I got up from the bench and ran to Abram just as he stopped his stargazing and turned to run back to me. We met each other with an eager embrace. Held close to Abram, holding him close to me, I felt everything must be right again. He and I, together . . . warm kisses, gentle words. It was almost worth the emotional storm to enjoy this glorious warmth and calmness.

We were in our own special world for a lovely while, then Abram moved slightly away. As I looked at his face, I knew that although his love for me was strong and sure, so was his determination to pursue the matter of our new lifestyle. He reached for my hand and held it tightly. He looked directly at me.

"Sarai, my own princess." His tone of voice asked me to be patient, to give him time to choose the words he must say, the words I must hear. What those words could possibly be I could not even guess. I thought Abram should have looked solemn and troubled, but instead, he was joyful, vibrant, excited.

When he did begin to speak, he talked on and on into the nighttime hours. Softly, with great care in choosing his words, he told of long, agonizing inner turmoil and of his deliverance from it. He gave me so much background for the day's climactic events that I was impatient with some of it. I realized he felt it important that I know everything he could tell me about his months of discontent and his tremendous victory. I listened with increasing amazement. He had experienced uneasiness about worshiping the gods of Ur long before the day of my outburst.

"Sarai, your brave, wildly expressed rebellion against temple rituals was a catalyst for me! Before that day I was trying to overcome my restless feelings by increasing the time I spent at the base of that ziggurat in prayer. But my prayers seemed to be in vain when directed to an idol made of metal taken from the earth. With heart, mind, and soul I longed to know a God of intrinsic power, of ultimate knowledge. I wanted a God who is alive, not a statue that had to be carried around. I knew there was such a God! I went to father Terah; he had often spoken to me of Him when I was a child."

"If he knew of such a God, why did he turn from him to Nannar and Nin-gal? Abram, how could he! And why did he not instruct us about the God he knew before he came to Ur? Abram, why?"

"I found this had been bothering him exceedingly! He understands his obligation to pass this knowledge of the one God on to his children. But he also knows one may worship this God only if one worships no other gods. This one God demands total allegiance. In the expediency of getting established and prospering in Ur, Terah conformed to local pressure and worshiped local deities. In doing this he drifted further and further from communication and fellowship with his God."

Abram paused for a moment, but before I could say anything he continued.

"We have spent many evenings in conversation about this God, and father Terah speaks of Him with such love that I know he regrets these past years. I have seen tears in his eyes."

"Can he not go back to worship this one God? Abram, might we worship Him also—instead of the gods of Ur? How do we worship Him?"

"Sarai, you can understand how I became filled with

longings to know Him. Sometimes I took time away from work to find a quiet place to think deeply about the God I was seeking, the God I knew was there.

"Then came the day of the new year ritual and your reaction to it. I evaded your questions then because my own groping for the truth and reality was far from over, and I could not advise anyone else at that point. But knowing your feelings gave me new urgency to know this other One. Gradually, my tortuous longing became ... anticipation! I knew there was a real, living God. There must be a way to communicate with Him. I prayed to this God!

"I had learned from father Terah that the God our ancestors worshiped was not made with hands as idols are. He is the Creator of all things, even the material used to fashion all the other idols. He is everywhere. The sky is as one of His eyes. He has all power and wisdom! He could cause an earthquake that would swallow up every idol of every nation — and then swallow up even the nations themselves! He can build mountains as high as he wants them to be. Once He sent water streaming from the heavens and rushing from beneath the floors of the seas so that there was a great flood high enough to cover every mountain He had made. Everything was destroyed. Mankind returned to the dust and clay from which they were made — except for one family he chose to use to replenish the earth."

Abram spoke in a crescendo, as though the pitch of his voice could convey some of the grandeur of his God.

I was relieved when he stopped talking. I needed time to allow my mind to accommodate the scope of the claims he had just made for this God. I am sure that, even then, we both realized the true wonder of the one God. There are no words to adequately describe Him!

There were tears in Abram's eyes, but they were not from sadness. His face glowed with pure joy.

After a few moments he spoke again, slowly and with great emphasis. He wanted me to realize the importance and the certainty of his experience.

"Sarai, can you possibly imagine this greatest God would speak to one man? Can you think He would offer that man the privilege of being His for a special purpose? He has a plan so great that I can't speak of it yet. I can only say this much — which is far too marvelous for my mind to grasp even as I tell you: This mighty God spoke to me! I am the man He has chosen to implement His plan!

"In return I no longer claim ownership of any of my possessions or even of myself. He has chosen me. He will provide for me. I am His. And He is mine!"

I looked away from him after he finished speaking, thankful he did not seem to expect an instant response. When I looked back at him, I sensed the solidness of his decision. I saw the calmness and joy it had brought to a man who had struggled and won in his quest to know the true God. He could give up everything and still be the victor. He was ready to leave occupation, city, house, old gods, family, and, if necessary, wife. It was as though his former life had ended abruptly. He looked the same. He was just as handsome, possessed with the same intelligence and ambition, but now he obviously was overwhelmed by his encounter with this God. His new faith admitted no doubt. He had met his God and belonged to Him — totally.

As future years proved, he did not always perfectly maintain that total surrender, but it was the main thrust of his heart, soul, mind, and strength. He knew his surrender to God was the channel of guidance, renewal, comfort, joy and strength.

I knew if Abram had known such a shining and dynamic moment of encounter with God, no words of mine, no former desires of his own, no obstacles of any kind would keep him in a place God did not want him to be. Nor would anything keep him from going where God called him to go. And I knew that the encounter would, from this moment on, shape his life and mine.

We had been silent for a long while, but this time the silence was healing and strengthening. I had an inner peace I would have thought impossible a few hours earlier. There also was a strong inner opposition to that peace. It was a great fear of the future, which had suddenly become so uncertain for me. Two beautiful thoughts sustained me and overcame the opposition: that I would not be separated from Abram, and that I, too, wanted to learn to know this God who speaks to a man; I wanted to share in the confident joy He had given His chosen one.

The first streaks of dawn were outlining the horizon in a silvery grey. Time had passed quickly, yet it had been with an essence of timelessness as well.

Abram stood up. Did I imagine it, or was he really taller than before? He looked across the garden and up to the sky, as if trying to memorize each blossom he could see in the light of the early sunrise and each star he could see fading into the lightening heavens.

"Sarai, I wish it were possible to describe my feelings when He spoke. I did rush home to tell you the glory of it, but in my excitement I said all the wrong things first. I wish you could hear the sound of His voice. There is no other sound with which I can compare it. But I can tell you His words and I want you to know them.

> Leave your country, your people and your father's household and go to the land I will show you.
> > I will make you into a great nation
> > > and I will bless you;
> > I will make your name great,
> > > and you will be a blessing.
> > I will bless those who bless you,
> > > and whoever curses you I will curse;
> > and all people on earth
> > > will be blessed through you.

We walked together back into our house. Everything was the same as it had been earlier that evening, but now as my eyes rested on each piece of furniture, each lamp, each pillow, carpet and polished vase, I saw them as hindrances to getting on with this fantastic venture I could not yet face. I prayed to Abram's God that He would help me relinquish my beautiful treasured things if that was how it really must be.

I went to my bedroom and walked out on the balcony. A soft, warm breeze was coming from the orchards. It made the torch near the archway flicker wildly. The flame was as unsteady as my heartbeat. I felt cool and came back inside. If only I could have been present at Abram's encounter with God!

The sun had risen now, and I had not slept at all. I looked out through the latticed windows to the vastness of the sky. Abram had said something about its being like the eye of God.

I went over to the bed and lay down. I pulled the cover over my face. In the darkness my mind could see all my lovely things. I pushed the cover back and looked again toward the sky, wondering if I could give them up for this God. If so, could I do it willingly and gladly, as Abram had? Abram had given up everything but me; we were still as one. That thought quieted me into a deep drowsiness, and I centered my weakening consciousness on him. The change in events had left him so vibrant and eager for the days ahead. Why could I not feel some of the same enthusiasm?

". . . to the land I will show you." Abram really did not know where we were going. But he was not afraid, and neither was I!

I was sleepy. I was emotionally and physically exhausted, and I slept dreamlessly for several hours.

4

... and together they set out from Ur of the Chaldeans....
Genesis 11:31

 hen I awoke, Abram had been gone from the house for hours. I knew he already would be in the process of resigning from his work so he could devote his entire time and energy to the many preparations that must be made. Since there was no appeal from the decision he had made, I, too, hoped to get done what I must do as soon as possible. There could be no joy in prolonging a difficult situation.

I was glad to have some time alone just then, for even after my morning nap I was moving and thinking as one in a daze, and I could do without conversation for a while.

After dressing and having a late lunch of fruit and cheese, I felt more alive. The first assignment I gave myself was to walk through our apartment, then through the entire house, then the garden and the fields and orchards beyond. It was to be a dramatic, self-pitying, solitary farewell before the actual harsh business of disposing of things began. When I came to an object of special value or of sentimental significance I would stop to look longingly at it, caress it. Then it seemed I could see Abram's face beyond each treasured item, implying that to be with him the possession between us would have to be given up. Probably Abram had similar experiences. But he would have seen the face of God beyond the object.

Midway through my melancholy trip my mind was flooded with words that crowded out every other thought:

I will make you into a great nation and I will bless you; I will make your name great, and you will be a blessing. . . . and all peoples on earth will be blessed through you.

I had only wanted to found a dynasty — God had spoken of beginning a great nation! I had only wanted to be a blessing to my people. God said He planned in terms of blessing all families on earth!

And would that not imply grand provision for our lives in order to bring all this about? How slow I was to begin to think of all I was gaining. Up to this moment I had been thinking exclusively about what I was giving up.

Then another marvelous thought filled me with a warm, delightful gladness. For us there would be no more Nannar and no more Nin-Gal. There would be no other God except this everywhere, all-knowing, most powerful one who did not demand any human sacrifice, and whose worship did not involve oppressive priests or orgies promoted in His name.

The God I was beginning to think of was a God of unique majesty and of great condescension. He ultimately ruled above all nations, but He would speak to one man and work through him in the world. And Abram had been chosen! Incredible! And I was to be involved, as one with Abram. Incredible!

I did not realize it then, but it was our God Himself who was giving me high thoughts such as these. He was ministering to my hurting self, easing my tight grasp on possessions. He was revealing a totally new quality of life, a life of abundant blessings I could not even imagine on that quiet day.

This was the first of many inner leadings that brought me to the certainty that as long as I kept my mind on our God and had real faith in His word — faith that results in even reluctant obedience — I would be given a peace which no circumstance on earth could destroy.

Most of what I learned of the life of faith was learned

slowly, painfully, and sometimes in accompanying moods of discouragement and depression. Abram, having come through his initial time of searching, had accepted the one God immediately as Sovereign. His dramatic response to God's call exactly suited his personality. If I had been granted such an overpowering meeting with God as Abram had, I probably would have been only thoroughly frightened. If Abram had to experience the gradual learning of God as I did, he would not have had the grand impetus to move quickly, leaving Ur and all it stood for. Our God knows each one of us so well, and fits His blessings and challenges accordingly. Beyond words of praise is our one God!

A sparkling wave of excitement began to erode my fear and residual anger. The more I thought of God's unique plan for Abram and me, the more I was fascinated. Just 24 hours earlier I would have been astonished at the mental calmness with which I let myself begin to think about sorting through our possessions.

That very day I began to make lists of what to take with us, what to give away, how to organize the formidable type of housekeeping which would be required in caravan living. It took weeks just to complete these lists, and I was able to postpone the actual disposing and packing of things for a while. The time spent in thinking out the lists saved valuable hours later and gave me space in which to accommodate myself to our gigantic transition.

As I had planned for the packing, Abram had been having long discussions with Terah. He explained to his father, as he had to me, about his being called out by the one God for a unique mission. Terah, when convinced of the actual message from God, was bursting with pride and joy. He agreed at once that to be God's chosen person one would have to leave the influences of Ur. And whether God had called him or not, he wanted to go along. And he insisted Lot must also go.

Terah always had been a man of quick decision, supported by quick action. He never displayed this quality more than when, having decided to move, he proceeded at once to liquidate his holdings in Ur. He used the proceeds to outfit a lavish caravan for the journey ahead.

Abram and I discussed Terah's reactions to our new calling with very mixed emotions.

"No one knows better than Terah how to bargain with the merchants and get the best provisions. We will live comfortably as we travel, Sarai."

"But remember the words God gave you, about getting away not only from your country and your father's house, but also from your kindred. Does this mean it is wrong to have father Terah and Lot included on our plans?" My words may have sounded like the voicing of a wonderful obedience to God, but they were only the voicing of a great fear. At that time, following God's desires was based more on anxiety about displeasing so great a one than of really wanting to do as He said.

"Terah is quite old. Nahor has moved to Haran, our ancestral city that Terah still loves, whose very name reminds him of the son for whom he mourns. With Haran dead, and Nahor too far away and too unconcerned to be of help to him, how could we leave him here?"

"But he wants to take Lot and . . ."

"Yes!" By the agitated way Abram interrupted I could tell he was questioning the same thing himself. "Why not take the boy? He has proved to be very considerate of his grandfather, and those two need each other. And, well, he seems to be much closer to me than a nephew, more like a —" Abram could scarcely say the word that expressed painful longing for him and for me—"more like a son."

That was reason enough for me to leave him behind! I did not want a constant reminder that we were childless and had to enjoy another's son. Surely it would be best if he and Terah both stayed behind. I had one more argument.

"Do you think Terah can stand the trip? He is not used to anything but comfort and ease now, and it has been a long while since he has traveled."

"He is as unused to inconveniences as we are. But he is strong and well. You should see him use his acute commercial skills to bring together the supplies we will need. I have been working with him on it all, learning much as I see how his rare combination of gentleness and shrewdness brings good results in business dealings. He looks years younger since he has been involved in this, and he is meeting every phase of the situation with poise and style. He will be fine."

I let Abram end the conversation, holding responsibility for taking Terah and Lot along. Really, I would not have wanted to leave Terah behind, for I had a feeling of security when this venerable old man was around. He had my admiration and love.

Dismantling our house and disposing of it meant many decisions and much work. At times both were difficult, but overall things went well and moved along almost too rapidly.

More than once I laughed at the astounded look on the faces of friends and relatives to whom I gave treasured pieces of silver, basketwork chests, carved furniture, and soft carpets. But they gladly carried the treasures away to stash them in their already amply furnished houses. They awkwardly wished us well in our tent life, and it was apparent they thought we had taken complete leave of our senses.

There was one carved olivewood chest that I allowed myself to use for personal items I could not part with. Into the box went an elegant soft white shawl, a pale blue tunic with embroidered borders of a deeper blue, several pairs of gold earings, a jeweled set of bracelets and matching necklace, an ivory cosmetic box filled with rouge, eye makeup, and perfume—trinkets representing a way of life that was at an end.

Actually we were relieved when our departure day came. It meant an end to the pressure of decisions, and it was a release into the one God's will for us. We considered it not so much a day of endings as a day of beginnings. We literally were stepping into our new life. We felt young and strong. We did not look back.

5

So he left the land of the Chaldeans.... *Acts 7:4*

*A*bram had given all the necessary information about our emigration to the government official who had replaced him as supervisor at the place of caravan entry and departure. Terah had settled the tax payments Ur demanded of an entourage such as ours. So, when our procession arrived at the city wall, we were allowed to move out through its massive gate with no delay. There was also no fanfare, no friends waving, not even much conversation among those in our group. We were aware of gradually leaving the familiar for the unknown — with full intent never to return.

Our caravan was not pretentious when compared to the great trading caravans that frequented this road. From the number of people in our train and from the modest clothing we all wore, no one could have dreamed of the wealth Terah was guarding in his saddle bags. Most of the proceeds from the sale of all our lands and goods which had not been used to outfit our caravan had been exchanged for rare jewelry and precious uncut stones. A lesser amount was in pieces of gold and silver, and in coins for use along the trade route. We were to trust the one God for our future needs, but I enjoyed the assurance of having great wealth anyway. I thanked the one God for having already provided for the future.

Although Terah was still nominal head of our clan, Abram assumed personal responsibility for each family member, each servant, and the children of the servants. He had assigned our places in the caravan with utmost care. He and Terah rode camels at the head of the procession. Lot and the leaders of Terah's servant-guards walked behind them. I, with two of my maidservants, rode camels next in line after the guards. We were followed by other female servants riding donkeys and holding small babies. Some maids were carrying baskets of provisions on their heads as they walked beside young girls who kept an eye on small children, making certain they did not wander off or get left behind. Next were male servants tending the pack animals and six strong porters from Luristan who amazed us with the weight they were able to carry on their backs. Last of all were the herdsmen and the flocks. In addition to our family members there were 65 adults and 8 children. We had a mutual respect for each other and, of necessity, a mutual trust in each other.

We inched along, not getting too far ahead of the slow-moving sheep. The miles per day would be few as we traveled through the luxuriant and flourishing countryside along the grand Euphrates.

Our trek along this caravan route would bring us, in time, to Babylon. Its very name was exotic! By the time we got there, would we be ready to give up the wayfaring life and settle in that city so famous for its dazzle? Or would we be content to keep trudging ahead to our mysterious destination? I knew Abram never would be content with anything short of coming to the land his God would lead him to; I was not at all sure what my choice would be. But, we were on our way — somewhere. I had never been outside Ur's city wall before. How endlessly large the world looked!

Our first day on the highway passed as though it were fantasy. I kept thinking, in spite of better knowledge, that we would turn around and go back to our house when darkness began to come. I never would admit to anyone such childish feelings, but they were very much a part of me.

We were glad many times for all the information Abram

had picked up from travelers about the highway. He knew where to find the best, safest places to spend the night. He knew how to find water for the people and the animals. He knew where the good trading centers were.

The sun was still suspended like a dull orange-red medallion in the hazy summer sky when Abram halted the group and directed us off to the left into a large open field. He allowed plenty of time to set up tents, get a good supper, and rest before beginning the second day's journey.

That first night of camping was a delight! Work assignments were carried out with no problems. Those responsible for the tents raised them quickly in the prescribed circular pattern. Other servants unloaded pillows, sleeping mats, and other essentials from the packs and carried them into the tents. The cooks prepared the evening meal. The herdsmen led the flocks into the fold that had been made by our encircling tents.

After our first supper on the road was over, a few herdsmen played pipes and lyres. The music was soothing. The air was soft and warm. We were content. The new life was good. We knew not all days and nights would be this easy and trouble free, but we thanked the one God that this beginning had been so.

For part of each day that we traveled Abram and I walked side by side. We walked leisurely, a habit that was foreign to us when we lived in Ur where we had been geared to a different pace. Now, the women caring for babies and the young children needed frequent rest times. The servants carrying baskets of provisions welcomed occasional breaks to put down their loads. The pack animals often wanted long, cool drinks from the animalskin bags. The Luristan men, for all their endurance, needed rest. And there was no way to prod the herds to move any faster. We soon realized we could be victims of dullness and boredom because of the wearisome slowness, so we made conscious efforts at conversation, bringing up topics which could be talked about at great length.

During these daily walks Abram and I grew closer to each other than ever before. We shared our superficial likes and dislikes, our deepest hopes and fears, and, although we did not dwell on it overmuch, we did speculate about what our home would be like in this still unknown place God was leading us to possess.

We watched the sky a lot and learned about clouds and all they would tell us about coming weather. We became interested in the colorful birds we saw, and if we didn't know their correct names, we would make up names for them. Wild grapes, pomegranates and date palms kept us from being too hungry between meals. We stopped to examine trees, bushes and wild flowers, admiring their design, color and fragrance. Abram often picked a few flowers for me to fasten to the veil I wore as protection from the hot sun and the windblown dust. We soon felt at home in the fields, under the skies, on the highway. But to be "at home" in its real sense was becoming a strange mingling of memory and hope.

Each adult in our caravan understood the purpose of our mission. Each person came with us willingly. Most of the servants had come with us out of loyalty to the family. I think especially of Abutab and Inmeshagga, who had been with father Terah since he had lived in Haran, and of the young shepherd, Neri, and his pretty wife, Lael, our best weaver. We could never think of them as servants—more as partners in our venture.

A few of the servants were eager to know more about the one God. In the evenings Terah would talk to groups of men concerning all he had learned from his father and grand-father about God. He talked of the great flood, of the dividing of people into many nations and different tongues.

The more Terah talked, the more he recalled, and the more he could talk. Each one who heard him was likely to pass along the stories to others and Terah impressed on them that they were never to add to or take away from the actual words of the one God as they were handed down from one person to another. It was a divine legacy and it was their privilege to share in it. We were glad young Lot had the opportunity to hear the record of God's working in the lives of his forefathers.

Knowledge of God increased in our group rapidly under so expert a teacher as Terah, and of course Abram told many times of his own personal knowledge of God. His hearers shared in his excitement with each telling of God's unique promise. Everyone in our household knew we traveled with a sense of divine purpose so we were like no other group on the highway. We were aware of the presence of the one God in a way we never could have been if we had stayed in Ur. Would it be possible to retain this fellowship if we went to Babylon to stay for a while? I really wanted to see Babylon. We could rent fields for the flocks, and the servants could tend them. We could find lodging in the city for a few days.

But we didn't stop at Babylon. Abram decided against even making a trading trip inside its walls. From the highway we traveled we could see its enormous wall and many tiled rooftops shining in the sun. There was one unmistakable towering hulk that absorbed our attention—their massive ziggurat! Abram said it was more than twice as high as the one at Ur. It was visible for a long time. It brought memories of our recently renounced city and of the reason for our renunciation.

We did stop at a small village some days later. It was called Sippar. After weeks of traveling during which we seldom saw anyone but those in our own caravan, Sippar was a welcome sight. There were several clusters of the black tents of the Bedouin in the wide grazing expanses around the town.

Our caravan stopped as close as possible to the well site. Abram and Lot rode into town to secure official permission to encamp there for three days. They were gone a long time.

A fear of the unknown made me wonder if the men of Sippar were barbaric—if they would hold our men for ransom! I went to Terah for consolation.

I didn't intend to show any fear, for ever since I could remember I had been taught to behave "like a princess" to live up to my beautiful name. It had been a personal, exciting game when I was a child—pretending to be royalty. It was my excuse to be impatient, selfish, self-centered, proud. It also had demanded of me a definite poise which I practiced long before I knew the meaning of the word. So, with a forced, sophisticated—perhaps childish—poise, I walked over to where Terah was resting in the shade of a beautiful grove of date palms.

"Father Terah, there is a marvelous breeze here, and isn't it fine to think we will be camping for a few days? We will all be glad for the rest."

"The breeze is fine, and I am certain the women and children need a rest, so we will stay here for a short time. As for myself, I am eager to get on to Haran. There are people I want to see there, and places I want to revisit." He had spoken in a casual way of "people" he wanted to see but he must have been thinking only of the family of Nahor. He had received little word from them since their move to Haran. To Terah's grief over the death of his youngest son had been added the sorrow of this estrangement from Nahor. Neither the tone of his voice nor the expression of his face betrayed his inner feelings. He also knew about poise!

"Yes, I will be glad to get to Haran, too. I have heard you speak of it often so I am very much interested in seeing it. And I will be happy to see Nahor and Milcah again."

I watched him closely as I said those names, but his only response was to change the subject.

"Abram and Lot are taking a long time in the village."

He had brought up the subject I had intended to talk about in the first place, and I pursued it.

"Why would they stay so long?"

"Observing the ritual of hospitality offered and accepted. Here, as in other villages, there is a central guest house. All visitors, shepherds who wish to let their flocks graze in the fields outside the town, caravan leaders who want to rest their people and animals for a while—all must go to this guest house to register. Before they can register, there is a get-acquainted time to help the local magistrates decide if they should accept the wayfarers or not.

"Abram and Lot will be presented to a council who will encourage them to talk—the longer the better—of where they are going, why they are making the trip and all they have seen on their travels so far. Then they will offer them the traditional drink of fermented sheep's milk."

"Ullp!" I had been attentive to Terah, imagining I was right there with Abram at the council, and my undignified interjection was a reaction to the "traditional drink."

With all semblance of sophisitication now shattered I stopped the small talk and got to the real questions on my mind.

"What if the men of Sippar don't believe Abram's fantastic reason for our journey? What if they suspect him of making up the story and think we are spies? What if they hold Abram and Lot for ransom?"

"Sarai, steady now. This is a good time to let your new faith get a little exercise. I will not respond to your 'what ifs.' Trust God."

Terah closed his eyes and tilted his head back against a tree. Just talking with him had helped me to relax. I was glad he ended our conservation without answering my questions with trite reassurances. His challenge to a greater faith was typical of him. It provided a loving, positive approach to the situation.

The day was nearly ended when the men came back from the village with permission to stay for three days. We had been refreshed from the afternoon's rest, and now we were eager to get the camp set up and the evening meal cooked.

At supper time Abram and Lot described the town and its people. Their reception at the town guest house had been pretty much what Terah had said it would be. The townsmen were friendly and helpful with suggestions about other places to stop along the way. They had not asked many specific questions because Abram apparently had impressed them well. I should have known he would.

It was comforting to have nearby neighbors for a while. It was good to know we did not have to pack up the tents and move the next morning. We slept well.

The wind rose high and shifted directions during the night, and I awoke to a noxious odor in the air. Abram had mentioned there was a bubbling tar pit close by. I had not realized how close! The smell was sickening. I now agreed with Terah—we should not stay here very long. We should be moving on to Haran.

Abram called a family council. Terah saw no cause to stay the three days originally planned. I was ill already from the smell of the tar pit. Lot always wanted to move on faster. Abram—I think secretly sharing all of our reasons himself— agreed to leave the following morning. Two days are better than three in such a place!

—*6*

...when they came to Haran, they settled there.   *Genesis 11:31*

I could not keep track of the number of days and nights between Sippar and Haran. Many of our waking hours were spent setting up tents and taking them down, packing and unpacking. We seldom stayed more than one night in any camp. The landscape was becoming more desolate now—no rich green forests bordering the trade route, few groves of date palms, few trees of any kind. There was an occasional field planted in cereal grain, but the crops looked sparse compared with the abundance in the fields we had been seeing. The animals found meager grazing.

There was a change for the better as we came to the River Khabur, a tributary of the Euphrates. We camped near the best fording place, and early the next morning prepared to cross over. Stream and river crossing was difficult. The animals hated it, and so did I. For some of the younger men it was a diversion they seemed to enjoy and they entered into a competition of urging the animals they were responsible for to swim faster and get across before the others. The men swam across when the water was too deep for wading; the women, children, older men, and cargo were transported on makeshift rafts supported by inflated goat skins and pulled with ropes which were in the strong hands of the Luristan porters. When we had to do this fording, the miles covered on that day were considerably less than normal.

We watched eagerly for Haran. A guard's first glimpse of

it was shouted for all the people to hear, and a responding boisterous cry rose from the whole caravan. What a welcome sight it was, this major stopping place for a crowd of travel-weary people.

Ur was separated from us now by a seeming multitude of weeks and by more than 700 miles of caravaning on main trade routes, detours and bypasses. We had experienced a wide variety of delays and assorted weather, but, in spite of that, and beyond our best efforts to make it otherwise, it had been monotonous. It had also been arduous work. We had every intention of making our stay at Haran a long one. The closer we came to it, the more excited all of us became. Since we did not know our final destination, this temporary goal was all the more an achievement to be celebrated.

Haran was a busy trading center, the hub of roads that led from Nineveh, Asshur, Babylon, and Ur in the east and from Damascus, Tyre, and Egypt in the west. It had been the scene of bitter fighting throughout its history. Terah had used many campfire sessions to tell us of its dramatic struggles, both military and commercial.

Now we had arrived and a three-generation delegation — Terah, Abram and Lot — went into the city to register our caravan. They had no difficulty obtaining the necessary permits. Their family was well remembered in Haran and currently was ably represented by the house of Nahor.

When the men returned, we were already beginning to set up camp. The work was done with more enthusiasm than usual and with more bantering and laughter among the workers than we had heard for a long time. Our meal that evening was elaborate by wayfarers' standards, supplemented by fresh fish Abram had purchased in town and by special bread Terah had bought at a baker's stall in the marketplace. The music after supper was louder and faster than on other evenings, and some of the servants sang and danced until the moon was high in the heavens.

Within a few days Terah contacted Nahor by special messenger and was overjoyed to see his son return with the messenger, eager to reestablish ties with the family. He extended an invitation for us to come to his home for dinner the next evening. I hadn't seen Terah so happy for ever so long, and he accepted the invitation on behalf of Abram, Lot, and me.

When the exuberance of meeting was over and the time had been agreed on for our visit to Nahor's home, he asked the inevitable questions, "What are you doing in this kind of a caravan? Where are you going? And why? What happened back at Ur?"

Both Abram and Terah were speechless. It was not that they did not want to share their marvelous news, but rather they hesitated jumping into it quickly.

They wanted to prepare Nahor for what they would be telling him. This was a story to be told with tact and reverence rather than in simple question and answer dialogue. I understood the reason for their silence and thought perhaps Lot's and my presence was making it more difficult for them to launch into their explanation.

I asked for the boy and me to be excused. I still thought of him as a boy although he was as tall now as Abram and had been learning from the Lurs about building muscle and stamina by strenuous daily exercise. He and I walked companionably through the camping area and across some of the beautiful pasture land. Lot was interesting company. He evidenced a good knowledge of shepherding in his comments to herdsmen we passed, and his personable way of speaking to them was a gracious talent.

When I got back to my own tent I was glad for the luxury of an afternoon rest. Imagine! Sleeping in the middle of the day! It was wonderful.

I awoke when Abram returned to the tent after taking leave of Nahor. He knew I would ask, and I did, "Did you tell him? What did he say?"

Abram's expression was impossible to read but his voice implied disappointment. He gave a very unemotional resume of the discussion.

"Nahor was impressed. He was convinced. But, Sarai, he is glad the one God chose me and not himself, for he is involved in pressing personal affairs and could have paid only minimal attention to Him.

"Then too, Haran is in Nannar and Nin-Gal's province, and while he headquarters here, he is required to give them prescribed honor and sacrifice."

"Did he make you doubt your own decision, Abram?"

"No—NO!"

The next day I was preoccupied with getting ready to visit Nahor and Milcah. I bathed and washed my hair, and Talmai braided it for me. I put on my sky-blue, ankle-length tunic, my largest gold earrings, my bracelets, and my jeweled sandals—all of which had been packed away in that special chest Talmai carried for me. I was looking forward with delight to a fine meal, served in style, accompanied by stimulating conversation.

Abram paid exceptional attention to his appearance, too, even trimming his beard. He wore his best white robe and his finest leather sandals.

Terah looked the part of a wealthy sheik, and Lot—much more elegant that I had ever seen him—had seemingly turned into a prince! Nahor would be proud of his family this night.

By late afternoon our camels had been saddled, and our attendants were ready to escort us to Nahor's house.

It was a fairly large estate, and one glance told us that Nahor and Milcah were prospering in Haran.

"I have become one of the leading merchants here very quickly—in the family tradition," Nahor said in answer to our profuse comments about his splendid house.

Milcah and I had our own private conversation while the men talked, but, suddenly aware of a lull in what had been a steady flow of words between the host and his guests, she turned to the men and said, "Our house is large enough for us all. Will you stay with us while you are in Haran?"

"Thank you, but I think not." Terah's answer was so ready that we knew he had considered it in advance. "Of course we will want to see you often during our stay here, but we must not get too comfortable at any place until we arrive at our destination. If we did, we might be tempted to stay on and on."

Father Terah had spoken for all of us.

Abram advanced another reason for declining their hospitality. "We have a responsibility to those in our caravan. We are more like a family than masters and servants. They are new in their faith in God and need encouragement. Our place is with them—to implement the closeness we all feel to each other and to God."

The fleeting imagery that had flooded my mind—of pampered ease in this city mansion—was gone. I knew Terah and Abram were right. I wished it could have been otherwise.

Milcah quickly turned our conversation to a lighter vein, and we continued to enjoy each other's company until quite late that evening. Then we said a heartfelt thank-you and a goodnight and went home.

Just before I went to sleep, I said, "Two or three weeks in their home would have been nice."

Abram didn't answer immediately. Then with great care in choosing his words he settled the topic once and for all. "When you make a sacrifice, even to an idol, you do not take part of it back. I, and my household—of their own free wills—are given to God. His instructions are to leave city, house, and kindred."

"But we didn't leave Terah, and we didn't leave Lot."

"I know. But they are at least one with us in spirit. They have left their home.

"Sarai, perhaps it would not have been wrong to stay

with Nahor and Milcah for a while, but their way of life could have become a stumbling block to resuming our pilgrimage. My dearest, I don't want to deny you any pleasures, but I must keep our priorities in line."

He spoke with an understanding that eased the lingering disappointment I had. I was totally in love with my husband. Mansions were incidental. Anyway, as Abram said, we were pilgrims going through a time of disciplining. Soon we would receive—on behalf of all mankind—blessings from God. Suddenly that thought seemed ironic. We were the chosen people. Why were we in a tent? We didn't even know where we were going! We had no idea of when God would even tell us. We had no family of our own.

In a confusion of loving Abram, wanting to obey his God yet doubting Him, coveting a lovely home, and grieving for unborn children—I felt the tears come. This is not the way our beautiful evening was to have ended.

I tried to pray to Abram's God. In the dark, in the stillness, with Abram already asleep beside me, I prayed. I prayed my hopes; I prayed my doubts. I prayed for faith like Abram's. As I stumbled through awkwardly worded prayers, I felt a calmness settle over me and with it an unmistakable sensation of gentle joy. This is how God answered me. It was not a direct encounter, as He met with Abram, but it was just as real! I had spoken of Him before as Abram's God, as the one God. Now I could speak of Him as my God. The evening had ended well after all, very wonderfully well, I smiled with my heart, closed my eyes, and slept until morning.

"Good morning, Sarai."

"Good morning, Abram. Tell me, does God seem closer to you when you have absolute faith and are in total obedience to Him than He does when you have doubts and when you have not wanted His will in all things?"

"What a profound discussion to begin so early in the

morning!" Abram registered bewilderment and then he laughed heartily. "All right, let's talk about it. To answer in a rather few words—although I welcome opportunities to speak at length—I would say God is always close. And I have never had what you call 'absolute faith.' I have never yet been in 'total obedience.' These are goals but not realities for me; they may never be.

"I think we are more aware of God's closeness at certain times, but that does not mean He ever leaves us. Prayer is one way to enhance fellowship with Him. That is why I often go off by myself for hours at a time—just to concentrate on His nearness, just to talk with Him. It sounds mystical but it is quite practical."

For the first time I had something to contribute to such a lofty discussion. "I talked with God last night and He answered with joy and peace. He and the joy and the peace are real!"

Wondrous moments like these, sharing with each other about God, became frequent. We encouraged each other, praised our God, then went out from our tent to the day's work.

We were comfortable in Haran and we looked forward to being there for the next few months. Our flocks needed a long rest and time to regain weight. Many animals had died along the way. We had to stay in one place until the flocks could be replenished with new lambs. Pasturelands were better here than any we had passed by recently, and there was plenty of water.

Our neighbors in the grasslands around Haran were both Bedouin and Aramean. Our women became acquainted with their women as they gathered at the well, morning and evening, to draw water. Our men became acquainted with their men as the shepherds brought their flocks in to water them at the earthenware trough beside the well. Both drawing water and watering flocks were essential tasks, not only because they supplied specific life sustaining needs, but because they provided an opportunity for conversation, gossip, and social diversion.

From our camp we could see the large fortress at the city wall. We went past it many times in our trips to Haran to buy and sell. We enjoyed the marketplace filled with stalls of produce, honey, wine, freshly caught fish, fine spices, bread, and staples like salt and corn. Zaccur, one of our most trusted servants, was in charge of bringing the wool from our flocks in to market and getting the best price for it.

Haran's streets were lined with brick houses shaped like beehives. They were well built, but their lack of style and beauty was in laughable contrast to the homes of Ur—and to the great house of Nahor out on the edge of the town. These typical Haran houses looked as though they had grown out of the earth from seed planted in rows. Their bricks were the same dull brown color as the ground.

One day at the invitation of a merchant Abram had become acquainted with, we were invited to visit him and his family in one of these "beehives." The interior had two rooms, whitewashed walls, and floors covered with an array of brightly colored rugs, cushions and bolsters. There were two windows to let in the light and a hole in the center of the rounded ceiling. Our host explained this hole was to allow smoke to escape, and the domed ceiling provided some coolness in the summer. The thick walls kept the warmth in during the winter season. The merchant and his wife were proud of their home. We often stopped by to talk with them when we were in the town, and we grew fond of their little home, too. We felt more comfortable there than we did at Nahor's home—perhaps because it did not pose any threat to us.

In spite of the marketplace treasures we found and the warmth of our new acquaintances, our trips into town were somewhat depressing because we were confronted with a materialism and moral decadence that we thought we had left forever back in Ur. And looming over the whole landscape was the temple, dedicated to the same deities that demanded homage at Ur. The same ritualism and system of sacrifice was observed.

We made no sacrifices to them, of course, but we noted the splendor of the temple with regret. We could not have so fine a temple for our God. He had no temple at all. When we talked of this in one of our early morning sharing times, Abram and I decided our longing for a temple for Him was really a longing for something tangible for ourselves as we prayed and worshiped Him. Most certainly that was why He never directed us to build a temple for Him. He was teaching us that His presence is not confined to a place behind man-made walls.

No visible place of meeting, no audible messages now — we were certain He was with us, but we were concerned about the absence of further commands, leadings, promises. The concerns, for me at least, grew into questions about what could be blocking communication. Having come this far we must not let anything or anyone keep us from Him. I was haunted more and more by what Abram had said about our being required to leave our "kindred." I still worried — could having beloved Terah and young Lot with us be a violation of that?

Heaviest of all was the wondering why I was still child-less. Abram and I were almost beyond the age to have children. God's commands are absolute, and so are His promises, and one does not doubt absolutes. And yet — how could one not see prolonged delays as denials? Negative wonderings encroached on too many of my waking hours, bringing moods of restlessness.

"Abram, when will we leave Haran?"

"Are you not comfortable here?"

"Yes, but..."

"Is there a greater thing we could be doing than waiting patiently until God shows us our next path? If so what would it be?"

Abram's responses were not really the answers to my questions, but they made the questions seem unimportant.

We had much to learn about patience and faith. Really, we were learning about patience and faith each day—but it felt more like frustration at the time!

7

After the death of his father, God sent him to this land . . . .   *Acts 7:4*

*A*bram began to spend more and more time alone in the hills beyond the pasturelands. He called this his "waiting before the Lord." No one intruded on his solitude, but from a distance many of the servants, Lot, Terah, and I prayed for him while he remained in his vigil. We agreed with him in wanting guidance for the immediate future, not only to take us off this dead center of delay but also to verify that we had followed God's will in the first place when we left our homeland.

When he returned to camp each time, he knew we were hoping for an exciting message from God. His words to us varied, but their meaning was unchanging.

"God is real and He is with us. He is providing for us well here in Haran. Days and weeks are long to us but to God they are as a watch in the night. We need to praise Him for His goodness, and we must think great, magnificent thoughts of our everlasting, holy God. We can take His silences as well as His marching orders as tokens of His best planning for us."

Abram's enthusiasm encouraged most of us, but a few became more edgy by the day. They had come along, thinking to align themselves with a man who, because of his closeness to the one God, could provide quick success and security. So far they had not seen anything, materially, as good as what they had in Ur—and they were not interested in the history of Abram's family, or of their part in its future, unless it gave them an easier life.

Terah stayed in his tent most of the time now. Lot, to whom Terah would deny no possible request, could not persuade him to go for short walks. He said he was not ill, but he had no appetite. The choicest food did not tempt him to eat more than a few bites. One evening as Abram was sitting in the tent with him, he noticed tears in the old man's eyes. Terah looked out the door of the tent to the hills in the distance and said, "It will soon be time to leave Haran. It is best to travel in the spring when the grazing is good along the wayside."

"Yes, my father, that is right. But unless God tells us we are to move, we will stay on and enjoy the pastures of Haran for another season."

"When He calls you, I cannot go with you."

"Father! We will travel slowly, more slowly than before. We will make everything as easy as possible for you. You surely will go on with us."

"No. My strength is gone. You know that without my telling you. And I prefer to die here in Haran, the home of my fathers, rather than some place along the caravan route—to be buried in a field and forgotten."

Now there were tears in Abram's eyes as well. "My father, I promise you never will be buried in a field along a trade route. Do not even think of such things. Think instead of the land to which we are going, the land our God has promised."

"Yes, I will think of that, then I will sleep."

Abram stayed beside him several hours after that bittersweet conversation, then went back to his own bed and slept until early morning. He arose and rushed back to see if his father needed anything or if he still was sleeping. He still slept, but this sleep was different. He would not need anything Abram could do for him, ever again.

Nahor and Milcah were summoned to the camp. They, and all of us, grieved genuinely at the passing of this beloved man. We could not imagine life without him.

After a time of mourning he was buried alongside his own father. A dynamic life had ended. A chapter had closed for us.

The necessary business affairs were handled as swiftly as possible. Nahor accepted his inheritance; Lot was given Haran's share; and Abram, being the eldest son, received the larger part of Terah's estate—the pieces of gold and the jewels left from the sale of his holdings in Ur. Abram's legacy was substantial, and we foresaw no problems in the time ahead if he handled the inheritance wisely and the wool trading went well.

He was faithful to his "waiting before the Lord" in the early morning hours. One day, soon after Terah's burial, he came back from his watch earlier than usual. The strains of worry over restless servants and the sadness over the death of his father no longer showed in his face. He saw Neri and Zaccur standing beside the baskets of wool ready to be sold in Haran.

He shouted to them in a voice that rang with rich laughter.

"It is time to move on! We will be heading now for Damascus, but our destination will be still further. It is to be in the land of Canaan! Break camp!"

Abram, now 75 years old, was head of our household since Terah's death. Terah had lived to be 205. His father before him, Nahor, had lived only 148 years. The family records showed that before Nahor the life spans were all over 200—Serug, 230; Reu, 239; Peleg, 239. Older records showed that earlier ancestors had lived much, much longer before the time of the flood. How often Terah had told us of these men, each one remembered by succeeding generations for particular feats of bravery and kindness.

The call to break camp was met with instant action. We were all in high spirits. The work began rapidly and proceeded well.

The morning of the second day after receiving our orders we were ready to move out. Nahor came down to see us on our way. He asked Lot once more if he would not rather stay in Haran with him. Lot, eager to see new places and to travel as far as he could, said a firm "No, thank you!"

With a dignity that spoke of his fellowship with God and of his resolve to follow as God led, Abram picked up a shepherd's staff and took his place at the head of the caravan. To my mind the staff was a royal scepter, wielded by a king.

Abram had sold the camels in Haran. He walked at the head of our caravan now, or at times rode on a donkey. I considered the donkeys for me and for my maidservants to be a welcome change for I had never liked the stubborn, ugly camels.

We must have looked anything but regal as we left Haran. Just another clan of nomads setting out for new encampments—so we would seem to many, but we knew we were different. We were chosen, set apart, called to be a special people for God.

For one intense moment as we left the site that had become so familiar to us I thought of the day we had left Ur. Memories flooded my mind so strongly that it seemed we might be on our way back there. But the idea had no substance. I knew we were going ever further and more permanently away from all that was past.

Abram and I felt an exhilarating sense of challenge, of mystery, of being in the center of a unique plan that, although not yet fully known to us, was cherished in our hearts. We were sometimes disappointed by delays and dismayed by circumstances, but we never felt Abram's call was unreal or misinterpreted. The difficult times just drew us closer to each other and to God.

Since Terah's death Lot seemed to belong more to Abram and me, and he was a joy to us. He walked or rode beside

Abram, and he took responsibility well.

Lot had a deep respect for Abram and was impressed by his uncle's store of knowledge. Abram, as a privileged member of the ruling class in Ur, had studied under the best teachers. He excelled in mathematics, astronomy, and geography. He had a basic understanding of the art of medicine. He was knowledgeable in zoology and botany. He was an avid reader when he had access to the extensive library at Ur. Getting the best information of his time was always important to Abram, but even in his early years he had an inner drive to reach beyond the sciences to their ultimate Source. And now this Source, the God of all creation, was his close companion.

Abram took pride in being Lot's teacher in these various sciences, but more than that, as he would have done with a son, he spent hours upon hours telling and retelling him of God. He talked of the creation of the universe and everything in it. He talked about man's initial sin and how evil had increased in succeeding generations until it took possession of man's thoughts and actions. He told of Noah's family who, somewhat like our own, had pleased God by faith in Him and was the family through whom God worked to restore the world after the flood. Lot knew well the sacred traditions that had been transferred meticulously from one generation to another. These precious accounts of God and of His people were not written on tablets of clay, as were those in the libraries of Ur. They were carefully preserved as one generation revealed them to another. God has a faithful remnant in each generation.

I was glad for the companionship we had with Lot, even though his being with us still troubled me at times. In one of my "wondering" moods I asked Abram if we possibly should send Lot back to Nahor.

"Of course not." Then, after considering the matter for a moment or two, he raised his chin a little, gave me a half smile and shrugged his shoulders. "Don't worry about it."

But I did worry about it. And I did pray for the son Abram and I wanted so very desperately—the son Abram was finding now in Lot.

It was springtime when we had left Haran. As Terah had predicted, the wayside pastures were green from winter rains. The weather was just right for travel by day, and by night the tents in the open fields were refreshingly cool.

The road wound around to the village of Palmyra. The mud houses there looked like those in so many other villages we had seen. Domed ovens were in use in the yards. Large water pots stood by each door.

We camped near some Bedouin nomads just outside the village. Some of the women in their camp were struggling to put up the black goat-hair tents. Others were carrying large jars of water gracefully on one shoulder. Their men watched, unconcerned. Bedouin women are so bashful that when strangers are around, they pretend not to see them. In courtesy, we pretended not to see them either.

Abram walked through Palmyra the next afternoon. He learned the town had suffered the loss of most of its animals through some sickness that had ravaged them a few weeks earlier. There were many hungry children, and there was little milk for them. He hurried back to camp and personally milked his favorite white cow. Then he and Lot carried the milk, along with twenty rations of grain, to Palmyra and gave it to the children.

This was not an isolated incident. He helped many people in many places. When they would thank him for his generosity, he would say, to their complete amazement, "My God has provided all this for you. Pray to the one God. Thank Him and praise Him."

We moved on to a small tributary of the Orontes River, stopping a brief while at a place called Riblah. There, the maidservants and I joined other women who were washing clothes in the sparkling stream. The beauty of the day and the excitement of being so near the border of Canaan made washing the clothes seem like a festival. We were getting ready for a stopover at Damascus, the last city before the Jordan River that we would follow into our land.

Damascus was a city I had heard about since I was a small child. It was legendary for its arts and crafts, its large-scale merchandising, and its inherent loveliness. It was situated on a high plateau watered by the Abana and Pharpar rivers. It was also famous as one of the major centers of Baal worship, and it boasted a spectacular temple site.

Abram halted our caravan near one of the seven branches of the Abana. As we rested on its grassy banks, he went in to make arrangements for our stay. We planned to camp there for several days.

The next morning, although he could have used some extra rest, he got up early to go into Damascus for a day of trading at the bazaars. Lot went with him.

I had planned to go into the city with Abram, but from what he had seen of it when he rented our camping space, he decided it was not a proper city for me or my maids.

When he returned, he had much to tell me about the exotic Damascus. In its bazaar were Aramean caravan travelers, Phoenician traders, and Hittite merchants. Abram bought some red, blue, and purple dyes, some spices, and bitter, medicinal helbenah. In addition to these things, which I had wanted him to get, he bought the usual staples and two unusual gifts. One was a beautiful circular piece of light tan tooled leather which we used for many years on the floor of our tent as a dining table.

The other gift was a new servant. Abram bought him but refused to call him a slave or consider him as such. He was a handsome youth, about Lot's age. Even a short conversation with him left one with no doubt that he was intelligent and witty. Abram said his previous owner was lavish in describing his capabilities and his ambition to excel in everything given him to do. His name was Eliezer.

Abram had not wanted me to go with him into Damascus because there was a great celebration honoring Baal. Every narrow street and all the large open squares were filled with noisy participants in the orgies that were customary at such a time.

"Sarai, I came away from Damascus awed by the holiness of our God who despises such degradation. One moment with Him, alone in the hills of Haran or in the stillness of my own tent, is enough to inspire lifetime devotion, and I am humbled that He has chosen me for His purposes."

At the appointed time we left the Damascus area. Our early morning departure through the plain to the south of the city was over a road freshly decorated with fields of pastel anemones, violets, and iris. Between the carpets of flowers were fields of grain growing to early maturity under the coaxing warmth of the sun.

The road came to a point where we were suddenly confronted with the most thrilling sight of our journey — a cascade of water from the icy slopes of nearby snowcapped Mt. Hermon as it rushed over the waterfall and splashed on giant rocks below before settling into the River Jordan. When I saw its lively sparkle and swiftness, my heart ran with it down the watercourse into my new land!

The road followed the route of the low-lying river, past Lake Huleh, on to the Sea of Kinnereth. Our people grew quiet as we came down the trail into this valley.

The shimmering blue of Kinnereth entranced us all. This jewel was nestled among tree-covered rolling hills, large vineyards, terraced fields of grain, and breathtaking stretches of poppies, daisies, chamomile and storax blossoms.

This — and more — was to be our homeland!

"Sarai, never have I seen such perfect natural beauty! And it will become even more beautiful and productive as it is tended by people led by the one God, people who will love this land with a uniquely keen passion."

"Will we stay here, Abram, in this lovely place by this quiet sea?"

"No, we will travel through the land. We must see it all. And I want to reach a very special place I have heard of—near a spectacular oak—before we think of stopping for any length of time."

We did stay on a flower-covered hill overlooking Kinnereth that night. The next day we reluctantly left—hoping to return.

A few days later, Abram stopped our caravan in a large open space with no city near. It was open camping here, and the general rule in Canaan was that one could freely camp in open fields but must defend it himself if someone else wanted it. We settled down, feeling we belonged and no one would drive us away. I wanted to stop traveling. It had been almost a year since we left Haran.

Abram slowly scrutinized the landscape in all directions. His eyes brightened as he saw one especially magnificent oak off to the right. Alone, he walked over to it and knelt under its branches. He was there for a very long time. When he returned to us, his face was positively luminous!

"The one God has appeared to me again! This is indeed the land God has promised to us. We have arrived!

"And Sarai, He again promised us children. He said—" Abram paused as if it might be sacrilege to repeat the words of the Holy One. "He said, 'To your offspring I will give this land.'"

The incredibility of His reaffirmed promise of children yet to be born to Abram and me and the glorious sight of the land given to us—overwhelmed us. We were each pre-occupied with our own thoughts and our own praises to God.

After a while Abram spoke again with a reverence in his voice, "I recognized that great oak as the Oak of Moreh. Travelers from this area speak of it with awe, and no wonder! Look at its size—the spread of its branches! Some people worship it as a god.

"When I walked over to it, I thought of its Creator. And He was there! He spoke to me only briefly, but I stayed there a long time before coming back to rejoin you and the others. I wanted to fully absorb the glory of that moment so that I would never forget it, never doubt that my God is with me — caring and knowing how to lead me to what is best. Before I left that place I built a stone altar. There is more love, adoration and faith represented in those stones than in all the bricks, jewels and gold of the temples to Nannar, Nin-Gal and Baal. And it is a different kind of love, adoration and faith, for it is directed to a different kind of God. Our one God, He is God!"

8

From there he went on toward the hills east of Bethel and pitched his tent, with Bethel on the west and Ai on the east....Then Abram set out and continued toward the Negev. Now there was a famine in the land....   *Genesis 12:8-10*

We camped near that oak for several weeks. I remembered our first night as though it were last evening. I looked out from my tent to the other tents set up in a protective circle for our flocks. The next nights the herds would be gone, sleeping in pasturelands where our herdsmen would guide them during the day. It looked so peaceful in that starlit moment, part of a familiar pattern. I smiled to myself as I thought of how totally unimaginable and impossible this kind of life had loomed in my mind when I was first confronted with it. My two reactions then were anger and fear.

The fears had faded, and so had the anger. How was it possible to have changed this much? As I stood in the door of my tent, I indulged in long thoughts about it all.

My love for Abram and my desire to please him had been part of the motivation for my change in temperament, but that was not the whole answer. The real reason was sweetly, wonderfully clear in my mind, although I had no words to express it then. Even now I long for transparent words to allow the meaning behind each one to show through. Almost imperceptibly I had fallen in love—a pure and devoted kind of love—with the God of Abram!

It was first through trust in Abram that I believed at all in

Him. I knew Abram never would have made up such a story. As often as he told it, his account never varied. He made no attempt to alter it for those who would only scoff or doubt his sanity. His was a God of reality and truth, and as he told of his faith in this God, I began to believe in Him also.

After I rejected the gods of Ur, there was a place in my heart that would fill with a restless longing. When the longing would leave, there was in its place a numbness like death.

The God of Abram had steadily, imperceptibly, gloriously filled that place. The God who rejects human sacrifice and oppressive, contrived rituals, whose creation is the world and every creature in it, who loves all nations enough to want to bless them—this is truly God! Sheer amazement that this God planned to use Abram and me in His way to bless "all peoples on earth" had gripped my mind.

There were still more mysteries than there were answers, but on that beautiful night the lingering doubts were weak enough that I would have told the whole world that, indeed, I did have faith!

Day followed day at Moreh, and I wondered when Abram would receive instructions to settle down in a chosen place in Canaan. We could begin setting up a village that would, under the providence of God, grow to be a town and then a city. It would be the headquarters for implementing the divine plan which was still beyond our comprehension.

Meanwhile, there was always work to do. I had taken more and more of an active part in the chores that were the women's responsibility. I enjoyed doing a share of the baking, churning, and mending. As we worked together, we would talk about how we felt, how we liked the weather or didn't like it. We sometimes talked of our husbands, and the more fortunate women spoke of their children. We would reminisce about places we had been and share our impressions of Sippar, Haran, Palmyra, the Sea of

Kinnereth, and other interesting sights and stopovers. Time went quickly when the conversation was good.

Neri and Lael's first child was born while we were at Moreh, and I attended her at the birth. The baby was a precious little girl—a perfect blend of her parents' handsome features. Abram took a lamb to sacrifice at the altar in thanks for this child who, from her earliest days, would learn of the true God.

When Lael was strong enough to travel with the baby we moved from Moreh to a place between Bethel and Ai. I hoped that would be the location for our city. It was not. But Abram built an altar there and spent part of each day waiting before his God in quietness and coming away with an obvious joy and serenity.

Gradually, we moved south toward the Negev. The measure of faith I claimed that first night at Moreh was ebbing, and in one of our early morning times of talking together about God I decided to let Abram know how shallow his wife's faith really was.

"I can't have real faith when I doubt so often. It is a total contradiction! I am discouraged. I never will have real faith!"

"Sarai, doubt is not the opposite of faith. I don't suppose anyone has ever had faith with no doubts.

"You have more faith than you realize. Not to have any faith in God would have meant to refuse to leave Ur. It would have meant staying there, serving false gods and piling up things to try to make life worth while. Not to have any faith would have been to stay in Haran where living was comparatively easy and we could have been with our family.

"My dearest, we have been obedient, both of us, even when our human nature wanted us to take a different course. We have, in the world's eyes, given up much. That takes faith.

"Sarai, would you want to go back?"

"No! No, but I am nettled with doubts. I don't

understand the need to travel so far and to move so often. I don't think I can have a child after all these years!"

Mentioning the lack of an heir was certain to devastate Abram's faith if anything could. He was quiet after my deliberately cutting words. But I had not disturbed his faith at all; he was merely thinking of how to reenforce mine.

"Sarai," he began, and his eyes glistened as with a knowledge of a wonderful secret he was about to share. "If a dear friend came to me, in love, asking how something I had promised actually could be so, I would not think that person lacked faith in me or did not respect me. I would try to explain matters to him, or else tell him he shouldn't bother his head about it, for I would see that it came out all right.

"Lack of faith would mean not coming to me at all. Honest questioning and explaining would draw us closer to each other."

"Then I will call my doubts 'questions' and refer them to God. At least I will try."

"Even trying is faith! And Sarai, keep your mind on the one God more than on your disappointments and troubles. There is real, vitalizing peace in thinking deeply of Him and keeping aware of His presence."

"Abram, it sounds so high, so mystical. But I know you are right." I started to sigh but the sigh was usurped by a gale of soft laughter.

"What are you—" Abram looked startled, almost frightened by my sudden change of face and mood.

"Oh, I was thinking of how it would be to tell the people of Ur or Haran some of the things we have been talking about this morning. I can't think of it and not laugh. Imagine telling them that doubting is faith; that material things are just passing illusions; and that spiritual things are the only reality!"

Now Abram laughed, too. "They wouldn't even listen to us. But for now that is beside the point. It is not what they would say or think, but whether you believe all you have just said. If you do, you have faith, Sarai!"

"I do believe all I have just said, and I want to believe it even more surely."

"We have shared important thoughts, Sarai. I thank God for you. It makes my own faith stronger as I share it with you."

It was time for words to stop so we could think about the ones already said, and so we could attend to things that demanded our attention that day.

The pasture lands were turning brown and we were preparing to move further into the Negev. As the season remained hot and dry and grass became increasingly sparse, we went even further south. At each place we camped Abram would build a stone altar—unadorned elegance—to God.

Although we were finding the southern part of Canaan in serious drought, it was useless to think of going back to the north, for we learned from herdsmen coming from there that drought was a problem everywhere in the land. The abundant spring rains had not come. The people faced famine within a few months. Shepherd people, especially, lived primarily on what was currently produced. They stored only enough to get the family through the winter. Canaan was not a land of storehouses. Individual families did not have facilities for long-term piling up of life's necessities.

The word famine struck my mind like a dagger. I had heard of famines but could not imagine being in a place where one would affect me. And I could not imagine God's leading us to such a place! Anxiety crept into my mind and gnawed away at it so steadily that it could not be shrugged off. It grew into fear.

Our moves now were hard going for us and for our animals. We had to face the fact that the season for spring and early summer rain had ended. The ground cracked under our feet. Blowing dust and sand was more than an annoyance. It became a threat to survival. We stayed inside the tents most of the time, out of the sun and away from as much of the hot winds as possible. There was no doubt that we were in trouble.

The staples we needed to purchase were becoming outrageously expensive. Shortages and projected shortages allowed merchants to demand more for their wares. It also caused people to try to buy more than normal amounts in case there would soon be nothing left to buy. The wealth inherited from Terah and the profits from our herds, while still ample, were diminishing more rapidly than we could have thought possible.

The servants came to Abram with questions arising from doubts about his leadership, and about his God.

"Why has God led us into famine?"

"Will He intervene with blessings? When?"

"If He does not intervene, can we go back to Haran?"

"What about going back to Ur?"

Abram looked steadily at the leaders who had come to him with the questions of our people. It was a look of love mingled with sadness, because he had no easy answers for them.

"I, and my wife, Sarai, and my nephew, Lot, will not return to those places. We will not go back. What our God has promised, He promises yet. As for the famine, I cannot tell you when it will end. I want all of you to stay with us, but that choice will be yours. There will be a special campfire this evening. Ask all the people to be there."

As the men walked away from the tent, Abram came inside and sat down, looking weary and older than he had only a few hours earlier. I poured him a glass of water and placed a bolster and some cushions at his back. He leaned on them, eyes closed, sipping the water.

"Sarai, I will not want any supper. I am going to seek the sweet presence of God. The doubts of men, the discouraging attitudes they live with, the despair on their faces drain me. I must see my God for renewal. One glimpse of Him, one word from Him, and I am refreshed."

My heart ached for my husband that afternoon. He felt a responsibility for our people, not just in providing food and other necessities for them, but in strengthening their faith in God.

Abram had directed our group to a large oasis. It was famed for its bountiful grass, trees, vegetables, fruit, and grain fields. It surrounded the excellent trading center of Gerar. We had come there knowing it represented our best hope, but it became just one more disappointment. The beautiful Besor River, which provided for its abundance, had diminshed to an ineffective trickle.

Abram came back from his hours of prayer just in time to arrange for the campfire. After relaxing around it for a while, we all began to sing familiar old songs. Abram led the singing, and his rich voice gave even the simplest folk music a splendid sound. After a while he stopped the choruses and stood looking at the group of servants who had thus far been so faithful and dependable. His affection for them all was apparent in his smiling face and gentle tone of voice. He asked for faith from each one — faith in him, but most of all a steady faith in the God who would provide. He spoke with an engaging joy in his voice and with a contagious confidence. They received his words well, and in almost childlike expectancy they waited a few more weeks for the miracle of rain, some direction of where to go, some communication from God. None of these things happened. The undertone of grumbling began again.

Hot and dry by day, very cool and dry by night. Wind both day and night! The flocks were finding almost no nourishment in the parched fields. We had enough to eat but we felt our restless, unvoiced concerns. We did not want to admit lack of faith, but we could not admit the presence of hope.

One family decided to leave us. Abram allowed them to

go, but not before reminding them to keep in their minds all they had learned of the one God and to serve no other god, ever. He told them we would welcome them back if they changed their mind.

How many different places did we encamp in the wide expanse of that part of the Negev? Abram kept up a constant search for grazing lands to support the flocks. He made frequent, frustrating trips to trading centers to replenish our supplies. The search for pasture and for supplies became more difficult all the time, and we finally circled back to Gerar.

The situation was worse there than it had been when we left. The city was overrun with people who had come from the north on their way through this gateway city on the route to Egypt. Gerar was crowded with caravans, large and small. Tradesmen who still had wares to sell were asking prices only a few could pay.

There seemed to be no help in all of Canaan. Should we stay? Should we move? Where should we go? My mind was in a turmoil with the same questions our servants had. Eventually they haunted Abram also and drove him to a conclusion that surprised all of us. He decided we should go to Egypt.

"Egypt?" I could not believe what I had just heard. Had we come so far to our land, only to leave it?

"Yes, Egypt. Don't look so shocked, Sarai. So many others are going. We are right at the main highway that connects with the great Way of the Sea which will take us across the Wilderness of Shur to green pastures and abundance of water." Abram's words came rapidly but they lacked the luster of enthusiasm, and he finished his defense by saying, "It is quite logical."

When he announced his decision at the next campfire, two more of our original servant families decided to leave us.

They did not want the hazardous journey across the barrenness to Egypt. They were convinced Abram had no sense of direction or purpose now. They even doubted his God.

Having lost three families of servants, Abram knew he must replace them with other workers. It was not difficult to find persons who would join our caravan, but they were of different backgrounds than the families we had just lost. Around the evening campfires, when Abram would tell of his God and what his forefathers had known of Him—and of how miraculously He worked in this world—these new people had little interest. Their indifference influenced others who were wavering in their trust of the God of Abram.

Abram felt the mounting negativism and realized more delay would be deadly, so he plunged into immediate preparation for the long trek to Egypt.

"In all my waiting before the Lord these past crucial weeks, Sarai, there has been no direct guidance. I have longed for His voice, His presence—but there has been only silence. Even as I was planning the journey to Egypt, I would have been glad for God to overrule and direct me somewhere else. But since He has not, I believe we must go."

"Without His further command or permission?"

He ignored my question and proceeded with words meant to encourage his bold decision. "The route between here and Egypt will be filled with people fleeing from famine. It is only good common sense to go there for a while. And common sense is also a gift from God, is it not?"

I was too mixed up in my own mind about many things to try to answer his question. He didn't want an answer anyway.

Leaving the land where God had led us, without His expressed order, seemed wrong. Yet I could see no alternative. We knew Egypt had been a sanctuary for famine-beleaguered Canaanites many times. We would find plenty of food there for ourselves and our flocks. Our stay would be temporary. Why should it seem so ominous?

The morning we left Gerar we had no illusions about an

easy crossing of the land between us and Egypt. Even on the first day out we used the minimum amount of food and water. Conserving what we had with us would be our only way to survive the weeks ahead. Many of our animals died each day, and the ones who still lived became scraggly and walked even slower than their usual pace. They were no longer a source of milk for us as they struggled to survive. Both animals and people needed more rest each day in order to cope at all.

The days were fiercely hot, the nights mercilessly cold. The scenery one day looked the same as the day before. I wondered whether we were wandering in circles. I hoped not. Sand everywhere! Scrubby bushes and short grass grew from some of it. Sand everywhere! The wind blew it into our eyes, and we walked through it—ankle-deep, hot, gritty. Our scouts had difficulty finding water to keep our supply from being exhausted. I ached for the time each day when Abram would halt our caravan.

Our meager evening meal was the best part of the day, and after eating we would get to bed early for maximum rest in order to meet the challenges of the next day.

Before going to sleep I often closed eyes that brimmed with tears and cried, "God of our fathers, we are tired and hungry and thirsty. We are your people! Are we your people? God of our fathers, do you know where we are?"

...and Abram went down to Egypt to live there for a while because
the famine was severe.   *Genesis 12:10*

*T*omorrow should be the last day of our
traveling." Abram's eyes shone as he made the
announcement at the evening campfire. The stark landscape
had been giving way to heavier patches of grass. There were
more bushes and trees in sight from time to time now. We
already had noted these signs with some excitement.

"Do you know what part of Egypt will be our stopping
place?" The question came from Deuel, a shepherd who had
considered taking his family and leaving with the others at
Gerar. His voice had a sting in it, as if he were saying that
since Abram did not know where to settle in Canaan, he
most certainly would not know how to find a place of some
permanence in Egypt.

Abram ignored his tone of voice and answered his
question. "We will be going into Egypt at Zoan. It is a store
city in the land of Goshen, a rich city surrounded by very
large pasturelands.

"We will take a long rest there; our flocks can be restored
and allowed to increase. We will soon have wool to sell in
Zoan. Meanwhile, we have sufficient funds to go into the
city at once to purchase all the supplies we need. We must
thank our God for being with us through the wilderness. He
is our one God in this land of many gods. We are in Egypt
only for haven until the famine ends in Canaan. We will stay
here not one day longer than necessary."

Satisfying thoughts of plenty of water and food, a respite from traveling, and access to a great city swirled around in my mind so that even though I was exhausted, sleep would not come for a long time. And I was awake at the first light of day as it gently streamed in through the openings of our tent. When Abram awoke I was already up, beginning to pack our things.

In the last days of our stay in Gerar the stress of indecision about what to do in the face of famine had made Abram mentally preoccupied. He found a way to escape conversation by being busy about many things the servants could have handled quite well. He did not even save time for our one-to-one talks about God, and I missed that most. I had noticed he was not spending much time at the altar place in those frantic days. I wondered if God, who was still Abram's very life, missed that one-to-one time also.

Abram had, however, continued his habit of going over with me his plans for the immediate hours ahead. Perhaps it was a way of firming things up in his own mind. On all our journeys he had reviewed with me how many miles he planned to cover by nightfall. He would mention any towns along the way and speculate on their being good trading centers. Even on this present trip into Egypt, although there was not much to talk about in the way of towns or trading opportunities, he still told me what he could of the terrain ahead and of the progress he hoped to make. I was especially eager to hear what he would say of this day's travels and the goal we would reach—Zoan. He said not one word.

I had taken for granted his wonderful habit of sharing his plans with me. The wives of most other caravan leaders knew as much of their husband's plans as their sheep did. So I had to know about this day and attempted to draw out some comments about what to expect at Zoan.

"Is Zoan as large as Damascus?" I didn't care about the size, but this seemed an easy way to open the conversation. He didn't even hear me.

He paced back and forth in our tent, head down, hands clasped behind his back. Finally he stopped and sat down on a cushion close to where I was sitting. I waited to know the cause for his strange behavior.

"Sarai, Egypt is not like any place we have been before."

"I know—and it is more than a little exciting! Tell me all you can about it, and then let's hurry to get started. I want to see it for myself, don't you?"

Abram's face did not evidence the excitement mine did. He was thoughtful, almost stern. "Hear me out now. Egypt is a land of great wealth and power. The wealthiest and most powerful person in Egypt is its Pharaoh. He rules Egypt as a god. He is worshiped as a god. He makes and changes laws whenever it pleases him. He has power of life and death, freedom and imprisonment, for everyone in Egypt. He has a palace in Zoan.

"Sarai, he is obsessed with the desire to have larger harems of beautiful women than those of any Pharaoh before him. He has achieved that, so the reports of him say, and yet he is not satisfied. He has representatives at the city gates to watch for the most attractive women coming into the country and to secure them for him."

He had asked me to hear him out, but I could not stifle the alarm that streaked through me and made me physically weak.

"You don't think they would take any of our maidservants! You could not let that happen! They are like our own family."

"I don't think they will take our maidservants. I am told Pharaoh's idea of beauty encompasses more than youthful charm. He has developed a preference for a beauty that includes exquisite poise and intellectual keenness. Oh, my princess, it is you I fear Pharaoh's men will choose. It is you who would be the greatest prize for him."

I looked at him intently to see if this was a joke he was trying to tell. He could not mean that I—at my age, worn from an exhausting journey, dressed in clothes Pharaoh's servants would disdain to wear—that I would be noticed by Pharaoh's men at all, except in ridicule!

I couldn't suppress a smile, savoring what was to me a surprising compliment! Abram did think I was beautiful. He saw me as I was when I was younger. Oh, the sweet magic of love—at that time and since—has made Abram handsome in my eyes, too. I remember my instant delight that morning, treasuring the thought that Abram considered me attractive. It fed my vanity which had been starved ever since we left Ur.

He began speaking again, deeply serious. "And it is not just you for whom I fear. I fear for myself. If you are chosen, I will be killed at once. Pharaoh will not take a woman from her husband. If the husband is dead, there is no problem.

"This is why I must ask a terrible thing of you. I know you will be repelled by what I am going to ask, but please, first try to firmly grasp all I have just told you."

"It is in my mind, firmly. You are afraid I may be Pharaoh's captive and you may be dead. I don't need the question you want to ask; I am repelled by what I already know! Let's go back to Canaan, now. Do we have enough food for the trip back, or can we replenish our supply without taking the whole caravan any closer to Zoan? Why should we take such a chance?"

I saw Abram as I had never seen him before. He was terror stricken, and my emotional tirade was not helping.

"I'm sorry, Abram. I will control my fear if I can't do away with it. What is the question you wanted to ask me?"

He spoke without emotion, as if he were reading what someone else had written. I heard him without emotion, as if it were someone else speaking to a stranger.

"When the Egyptians see you and let it be known they want you for Pharaoh, say you are my sister in order to save my life."

At once Terah's face came into the eye of my mind. I

called him father Terah, as indeed he was; but I had always considered him more Abram's father than mine. He sired us both, but Abram was born to his first and favorite wife. I was born later to a woman he had taken after Abram's mother died. My own mother did not have the place at Terah's side that Abram's mother had, and although she and I lived in his household, we saw little of him. He had grown very close to his sons, especially Abram, and spent his time with them.

I was told when quite young that I would be given to Abram in marriage, following a usual custom. It was only after our marriage that Terah truly seemed like a father to me. Yes, I was Abram's half-sister. But for all of my adult life, I had been his devoted wife!

My mind had been wandering, refusing to face the present moment. Abram broke through my reverie. "Sarai, you are most beautiful. Pharaoh will want you. I know it. Will you save my life by saying you are my sister?"

"Yes! A thousand times, yes! It is true anyway! And you will find a way to buy me back or rescue me or .... oh, Abram, the Pharaoh won't want me! Besides, we have a nation to build; our God said so. It will be all right. Let's go on to Zoan."

Our caravan was on the road within three hours. We were in high spirits, most of us, and we let thoughts of the comparative ease to which we were heading fill our hours.

When the first sharp-eyed scout glimpsed the walls of Zoan and shouted the news, our people were ecstatic! We laughed; we encouraged each other to hurry; we did not feel tired any more. Our food supplies had lasted, and our stamina had met the challenge of the journey. With the wilderness behind us, we approached the city gate feeling not so much like refugees from famine, or reluctant travelers, but like soldiers who had overcome an enemy and were now ready to enjoy the spoils of battle.

At the point of entry everything was as Abram said it

would be. Our caravan had to be inspected carefully before we were to be allowed into the grazing lands of Goshen. A tax on each person and fees for grazing lands had to be paid. And there were members of Pharaoh's staff, intent on discovering any special woman who might bring diversion to the Pharaoh.

Abram left the caravan and went into the city's marketplace for provisions before he set off for the campsite. He took Lot and three servants with him so each one could secure different items and get the purchasing finished as quickly as possible. While they were gone the rest of us waited where our caravan had stopped.

I knew Pharaoh's delegation was watching me. I sensed their interest increasing. They began to walk toward me. I pretended not to see them, as I has seen the Bedouin women do when strangers approached. Behind my facade of cool detachment I was dazed with fear.

The spokesman of the group said, "You will come with us to that camel train over there to your left. You are to be interviewed by Pharaoh, and you are to be grateful for your great, good fortune."

"I do not wish such great, good fortune, nor do I want an interview with Pharaoh. My brother and I are here with other family members and servants. We have brought our herds for temporary pasture, but our stay in Egypt will be short. Pharaoh would have no desire to interview me."

"We will judge that for now, and later he will judge for himself. Meanwhile, we will prepare a large gift of camels, sheep, cattle, donkeys, menservants and maidservants for your brother, to express Pharaoh's appreciation for the company of his sister."

They were courteous, unyielding. There was no immediate help, so I did not make things worse by screaming, kicking and biting as I would have liked to do. With their permission, I instructed Eliezer to tell Abram all that had happened. I walked with them toward the despicable camel train—like royalty. I was glad Abram did not have to be there at that horrible moment.

I never could have dreamed of such an enormous palace! It was ornately filled with rich tapestries, thick rugs, colorful tiles, marble pillars, polished copper wall panels, domed ceilings lined with bright mosaics, and doors of gold. It was a jumble of ostentation, and, although I saw its overall grandeur, my mind was in too much turmoil to note its intricately detailed perfections.

I was led to the spacious section of the palace reserved for the harem, and almost before I knew what was happening, I was started on what apparently was an established routine for newcomers. First there was a perfumed bath in one of the several bathing pools. Then my hair was washed, dried, combed, and braided. There were garments of fine linen for me to wear with matching sandals. I was given a small luncheon of fruit and cheese and a glass of wine. After all this, my attendants allowed me to rest for a while. My bed was in a large alcove, curtained off from the rest of the very large salon where I had been undergoing a great transformation in appearance. I wished Abram could see me. I desperately wished I could see him!

The bed was luxuriously soft. I had been soothed by the bath and the food, and was now relaxed enough to feel drowsy. Half asleep, I tried to think what to do. There was nothing to do . . . but wait.

I thought of the weeks leading up to this as yet incomprehensible turn of events. Leaving the land God meant for us without His bidding now seemed so wrong. I wondered how we could have done it. His presence had not been as real to Abram, or to any of the rest of us, on our uncomfortable journey into Egypt as on our other migrations. There had been the weakening of communication between Abram and me, and then that sorry admission of his fears and the resulting cowardice that culminated in our using half-truths to try to outwit Pharaoh. We were enmeshed now in a situation from which we could not extricate ourselves. Dared I call on God now?

How had Eliezer explained my abduction? Had Abram accepted the gifts from Pharaoh's envoys? What was Abram feeling now? Had he devised a plan for my release? Dared he call on God now?

Somewhere in the midst of this maze of unanswerable questions I fell asleep. When I awoke the questions were still there—without solutions.

For the next several weeks my grooming process continued. There was a daily ritual of jasmine-scented baths. My hair was combed in different ways, and I was allowed to choose the style I liked best. My nails were buffed to a lustrous shine. Heavy ointments were worked into my hands, which had become rough from the daily work I had been doing. I was given a dozen changes of clothes, each outfit complete with veil, shawl, and sandals.

I was kept isolated from the other women while being readied for my meeting with Pharaoh. I had been given a private apartment and a personal maidservant who anticipated my every wish. She answered my many questions about Pharaoh's court. The girl was Egyptian but spoke several languages, including mine. Clearly she was a person with great talents and great ambitions. I had the distinct impression she felt I could be Pharaoh's next favored wife and, as such, would surely reward the one who helped me attain that position. She served me very well, but as one with a purpose beyond the immediate task. We got along well and I grew fond of her. Her name was Hagar.

For the ten months I was detained in the palace my life was a unique mixture of luxury, loneliness and fear. My heart ached for Abram. Talking about him was next best to seeing him, and I kept Hagar listening for hours as I told her about him and his special relationship with the one God.

Late one afternoon when I had just enjoyed a long nap,

Hagar tapped lightly on the door of my room and, at my response, came in. Obviously she had some exciting news for her eyes glittered like morning stars and her face had a becoming rosy flush. She was a beautiful girl, and, as bearer of great news, she had become radiant. I knew she wanted to speak, but I pretended not to notice at first, wondering if she would break the social rules and speak before she was spoken to. Her aura of high spirits was unmistakable, but she calmly poured scented water from a large container into a small marble basin, preparing to manicure my nails.

My curiosity would not allow me to play this game for long. "Hagar," I tried to speak with a tone of amused condescension, "what pleases you so?"

With a flashing smile of triumph she said, "In three days you will be presented to the Pharaoh. It has been decided that you are ready."

"I am not ready!" Ever since I had been in the palace, I had kept hold of an outward attitude of serenity and dignity. I would not be treated as just any well-favored woman Pharaoh's men happened to notice. I demanded and received a definite respect. But Hagar's news caught me off guard. In fact, because she looked so happy as she came in, I thought she knew something that would make me happy too—such as that I was to be released. When I learned her good news was my worst fear, I lost control. "I am NOT ready!" I said it again, this time with tears.

If I had lost control, Hagar had not. She assumed leadership of the situation at once. "You are ready. I have invested nearly a year of time and effort in you, far beyond what I was required to do. Now you will please Pharaoh, and you will reward me with many things I will tell you of later. I have watched you carefully, and I know he will want you. You will have power, position and wealth. Know what this means! You will have favor with the one who is god in Egypt! And you will remember the one who groomed you for this, will you not?"

She had spoken rapidly and softly. I knew she meant every word. She stepped closer to me and spoke even more softly—and determinedly. "And as you have talked to me of Abram, I have come to know he is really your husband. No one else in the palace realizes he is anything but your brother."

She did not verbalize a threat of betrayal of that confidence, but by this reference to Abram she was telling me she literally had power of life or death over him.

I looked at her for an intense moment, evaluating the strength that opposed mine. She had, for now, the advantage.

"I will want no supper this evening, Hagar, but bring in a bowl of fruit, some bread, and a pitcher of water. I also want you to see about a different veil to go with the aqua robe. The one you selected for it is too plain. I would like one with a few jewels in it. You can bring the new one to me tomorrow about noon for I intend to sleep quite late."

"As you request, I will do." Hagar assumed the attitude of a servant again.

We had each learned much about the other in the last few moments.

When she left my apartment I dropped down on a floor cushion, chilled to the point of trembling. I felt drained of life itself.

I cried out loud, "Abram, help me! Come to me!" It was a foolish cry, for I knew he could not come and he could not help.

Once more I cried, even more desperately, "God of our fathers, my God, help me!"

_____*10*

> So Abram went up from Egypt to the Negev, with his wife and
> everything he had, and Lot went with him. Abram had become very
> wealthy in livestock and in silver and gold.   *Genesis 13:1, 2*

I awoke early the next morning but stayed quietly in bed, not wanting to see anyone or talk with anyone. About noontime I arose, walked to the window, opened the draperies a bit, saw the sun was in its usual place and wondered why. Everything should be out of focus, upside-down, or backward at such a time as this. If the moon had been out I would not have been surprised!

In the early afternoon Hagar came in with my lunch. We did not speak. A bit later she returned with a lovely cream-colored veil, adorned with patterns of gold leaf and small white sapphires. Her taste was flawless, and I nodded a wordless approval.

As she left the room I called her back. "I will not need supper this evening and I do not want to be disturbed until I awaken in the morning."

Now she nodded approval. I thought she had an expression of apprehension on her face, and I foolishly believed she was concerned about having angered me by being so forward the previous day. Actually she had given that no thought at all; her concern was for something much graver.

Disregarding my instructions, the next morning she was in my room—early. She was not only in my room but she was pushing my shoulder, pulling at the pillow—getting me awake fast!

She ran to the window, jerked open the heavy drapes, and turned back to where I was lying. The sunlight streamed in, highlighting a dark-haired, olive-skinned, attractive young woman with eyes flaming in anger. She lifted her arms above her head in rage, then dropped them in helplessness. She had not yet said one word.

Then she began a slow, precise speech. "We had no time for conversation yesterday, and I would not have commented on it then anyway, but now you must know. The Pharaoh and all his family are desperately ill. The disease that is plaguing them began the day he decided to have you brought to him, and it has become increasingly devastating every hour since. He believes he soon will be dead and that his family will die too. He believes the plague has something to do with your being presented to him. He has sent for your Abram to try to find an explanation. Abram should be here by now."

Before I could reply she had run out the door. I would send for her again of course, but in the meantime I needed to adjust to what she had told me. Abram was coming here after all this time! At Pharaoh's invitation! At Pharaoh's command! I dared not think what might happen to him.

I closed my eyes to shut out as much of my situation as possible. In a different land, in a better time, Abram and I had talked of faith in God. We had discussed how thinking of our God's majestic power and holiness could bring peace. I concentrated on Him and on His promises to us. Our God would keep His Word. Our God created the world and everthing in it. His power extends everywhere. Yes, He could rescue Abram and me . . . . But would He, in the light of the way we had become involved here in the first place?

I felt too remote from Him to pray, but I knew He could read my heart with its yearning for His peace and strength and for His deliverance from this evil. I thought that if ever we got back safely to Canaan, Abram and I never again would run ahead of His commands!

I hadn't sent for Hagar, but she came back anyway and in a decidedly more agitated state.

"What is the latest news, Hagar? What is going on now?"

"I am to take you to the palace gate as soon as we can pack each garment you have worn, each comb, brush, and jar of ointment you have touched. Pharaoh wants nothing here that has been yours. He wants you gone! You are even to take me with you because I have been your personal maid."

She already had begun setting out things to be packed. Two other maidservants came in to help. Porters came with trunks into which they placed all the items—even the jeweled veil which I had never touched.

I walked over to the window without commenting, uncertain how my voice might sound and unsure of the appropriate words to say. I hoped Hagar would interpret the silence as a regal disdain for her abruptness. My heart began pounding so loudly I thought she must hear it, so I chanced a question and was surprised at the controlled sound of my voice. "Did Abram come?"

"Yes. His audience with Pharaoh was brief. He is already on his way back to his camp with pack animals laden with treasures from the palace. Pharaoh's personal guards escorted him away—as they will escort us out of the palace as soon as possible."

"And the illness of Pharaoh and his family, has it subsided?"

"It has. The fever and the pain are easing. This is all I know. I am under urgent orders to work as rapidly as I can to get this packing done, so if you will excuse me from further conversation I will give it my best attention."

I turned from her and went back to the window, trying to analyze all the emotions I was experiencing. Joy and relief—praise to my God—curiosity over what had happened during Abram's conversation with the Pharaoh—

and a dislike for the idea of taking Hagar back to Canaan!

The packing was finished quickly, and I could not help being impressed by Hagar's competence as she supervised the others and did much of the work herself.

"Do you want to go with us, Hagar?" I hoped she would say she didn't and that we could work something out for her so she could stay at the court.

"There is nothing here for me now. I will have no further opportunity to wait on a favored one again. My name is a curse to Pharaoh because I served you who brought to his house such distress. I am fortunate that I do not find myself serving the slaves who build the roads and the great public buildings—carrying water and taking them their daily rations! I most certainly will go with you."

"Then let us be friends, Hagar. Abram and I have no slaves, only servants, and the servants who travel with us are considered almost as family. We live in tents but we live well, and we live in an atmosphere of kindness toward each other as much as possible."

"We will be friends. I will serve you well."

She was an enigma to me. She personified bold resentment, and yet she looked somewhat like a frightened child. From the first I had thought she was a quality person, a step or two above the other palace slaves in competence, intelligence and beauty. I wondered how she had come to be a harem slave and not one of Pharaoh's wives. She could not have been born a slave. She behaved as one who had known both freedom and authority. In the years ahead I would get to know her better, but she never ceased to be a woman of mystery to me. She confused me. I felt as though I wanted to console and encourage her, but at the same time I felt defensive toward to her, remembering how she had used a shared confidence to intimidate me.

The porters took the trunks, and the delegation sent to escort us to the camp was at the door. Hagar and I were hurried through the most beautiful prison in the world, but my mind was so occupied with the freedom that waited beyond its doors that I caught only a fleeting impression of it — as when I had been hurried through these same halls on the day of my arrival.

Our camel train was waiting, and within minutes we were on our way. The camels moved with frustrating slowness, their harness bells tinkling incessantly as they plodded along. My mind raced ahead to my reunion with Abram. How would he look? What would he say? Not in all my imaginings did he look so handsome as when I actually saw him standing outside the camp, eagerly looking down the road as we approached. The obstinate camels walked still slower, but finally — finally — we were there!

We had a hundred things to say to each other and a hundred things to ask each other, but first we needed assurance that we were together again, safe and free. We ran to each other, oblivious of everything else.

Eliezer, never far from Abram when there was work to be done, had been standing a few yards away. He walked over to the camel train and began to direct the job of unloading. He had been told Hagar would be coming and arranged to have her escorted to the tent which had been prepared for her.

Abram and I were like young lovers after our separation of many months. We walked hand in hand in to our tent. We embraced again; we wept; we laughed. We held each other tightly, as if forever. We lost track of time. We were one again.

"Sarai," Abram had to face what he dreaded. "Tell me about all the time you were there."

"Tomorrow."

"Do you want to hear about my meeting with Pharaoh?"

"Tomorrow."

"Do you want to know about the gifts he lavished on us?"

"Tomorrow."

"Can you love me the same as before all this happened?"

"No, not the same—more!"

Abram smiled at that reassurance, then gently asked one more question. "Do you know God was with us and protected us in that place?"

"Yes, I know. And we will go back to Canaan, and we are still His people. Can we ever comprehend the greatness of our God? It will take a lifetime, won't it?"

"A very long lifetime, and even then there will be more to learn. What a legacy of experience with Him we will have to pass along to our children!"

With this good ending to our desperate circumstances, it was easier to believe God would yet provide the promised child. At this point nothing seemed impossible with Him.

We spent the next day telling each other of our experiences during the time we were separated. I told him of the elegance, the fine treatment, and the undercurrent of fear I had known there. I mentioned my new maidservant. I told him of trying to keep my mind on our God when I was most fearful, and of the strength He gave me to cope with situations as they developed.

Abram tried to describe his reaction when he realized I had been taken to Pharaoh's palace. He had rather automatically supervised the setting up of the camp, with the tremendous help of Eliezer, Lot, and the other servants. He did not eat nor sleep for the first two days, but constantly implored God for my deliverance and for guidance back to Canaan.

In the intervening months his flocks had been revived. The flocks Pharaoh had given him increased. His wool-trading ventures were successful. He had prospered greatly.

He told of his futile efforts to see me and of several attempts to get a message to me that would assure me of his loving, constant concern.

"Then," he continued his long narrative, getting more excited as he reached the climax, "a group of Pharaoh's men rode into camp before dawn. I was to go back with them immediately to see the Pharaoh who had become seriously ill, as had his household. I thought they had come for me because you, too, had caught whatever threatened the life of the royal family. I left with them at once.

"We arrived at the palace, and I was taken directly to Pharaoh's room. He was in bed, motionless, breathing heavily. With extreme effort he raised himself up on one elbow, leaned toward me and said, 'Ever since I have decided to have your sister brought to me, a ravaging plague has been attacking my family, and now it has come to me. Our physicians cannot diagnose it or cure it. Have you or your gods put a curse on us?'

"I cannot forget his gasping for breath, his labored words, the look of pain as he talked with me. I expressed concern for his health. Then I found the courage I had lacked before, Sarai. I told him that, although you are my half-sister, you are also my wife. I said I had been wrong in not allowing him to know the entire truth about our relationship. I even asked his forgiveness.

"He fell back on his pillow and, with all the strength he could call up, he said, 'What is this that you have done to me? Now your God is angry with me. Why did you not tell me she was your wife? Why did you say she was your sister? I might have taken her as my wife. Now! Take her and go your way!'

"Sarai, our God used the fearful plague to impress on Pharaoh's mind that there was a divine barrier protecting you from becoming his wife.

"He sent for his personal attendants and ordered them to escort me back to camp and to assist in any way to hurry us out of his country. He sent additional costly gifts of gold and silver.

"When we got back here, I did nothing but watch that road so I could see as soon as possible the retinue bringing you back to me. Eliezer went ahead with preparations to break camp, sending messengers out to the shepherds to bring in their flocks. He and Lot are doing very well in expediting things for our trip back to Canaan."

He stopped speaking, giving me an opportunity to ask a question or make a comment, but I had none. The tumultuous days Abram had just described were receding so fast they almost had a dreamlike quality already! Reality was here—the ability to reach out and touch Abram's hand.

Abram cleared his throat—I think to swallow a tear— and concluded his conversation. "We will be on our way in a short time, retracing our steps through the wilderness and back into the Negev. After a brief rest in Gerar I want to go back to the altar at the campsite near Bethel. We will never leave Canaan again."

With new energy Abram finished organizing the caravan's departure, and within a week we moved out. As I saw the speed with which everything had been done I continued to marvel at the deliverance our God provided to get us away from Pharaoh.

And just as marvelous as our deliverance from Pharaoh, so was the immediate restoration of our relationship. Any trace of bitterness toward him was swept away. His faltering and fears which caused us danger and heartbreak were gone.

And there was another wonder—our love for the land God chose for us had increased beyond belief. Going back to Canaan now was going home!

Best of all, our reverence for our mighty God had increased; so had our faith in Him.

11

Is not the whole land before you? Let's part company. *Genesis 13:9*

*T*he trip back led us through the same debilitating wilderness we had experienced nearly a year before. It was just as forbidding the second time. There were the deep-rooted acacia trees, sparse grass, and little else except sand, stones, hot windy days, and cold nights. The great difference was that now we were putting miles between us and the place we never should have gone, and we were coming closer each day to our land. We did not encamp anywhere along the caravan route for more than two days at a time until we reached a place in the Negev near Gerar. We found enough grazing land for our flocks and arranged to stay there until we and our animals were rested from our Egyptian interlude.

"Abram, we have been here ten days. I am quite rested and would like for me and my maidservant to be escorted into Gerar's market place."

The thought of going into town had been on my mind for several days. All the time I was in Egypt, I was in that palatial prison and had not been free even to walk through the palace, let alone to go into the city. Now the idea of browsing in nearby shops was a happy one.

"It can be arranged." Abram was smiling as he added, "I will be one of your escorts."

"Are you coming along to be certain I will not be extravagant? I well may be, but no matter. We are very rich now, are we not?"

I was teasing and had not meant to hurt his feelings, but it was clear I had done just that. He made no attempt to hide tears which filled his eyes and ran across his sun-tanned cheeks.

"It is good to have gold, silver, and flocks to produce even more wealth, but this accumulation of what we have reminds me of a part of my life I wish most desperately had never happened.

"Sarai, I left Ur willing to trust God for my total future and the future of my unborn children. This was a glorious, exhilarating feeling. I believed I was so near to God that my marvelous elation would never diminish.

"Does it seem sensible I could have trusted God for all that and not trusted Him for daily needs, even in famine?

"Fear drove me to look to Egypt for help, and fear caused me to lie outrageously to Pharaoh. I never can estimate what my lack of faith cost you in anguish, my dearest. I never can put into words the wild terror that possessed me while you were captive.

"It was fear, still supplanting faith, which motivated my accepting the gifts from Pharaoh. A great many of our animals had died before we left Canaan. A larger number died along the way, and the survivors were a weak lot. I knew we would be staying there indefinitely because I never would have returned to Canaan without you. His gifts represented a ready means to survive and prosper. So, again I used the excuse of 'common sense' and did the expedient thing.

"I have never seen flocks increase and flourish so rapidly! Never have our trading ventures been more successful than in Zoan! I did not have to worry about lack of sustenance in addition to the consuming anxiety of getting you freed and all of us back to Canaan.

"And now I have brought that wealth with us. My thought is that I should send it back to Pharaoh—send back all he gave me with interest!"

He looked at me questioningly and waited for me to speak. Did he want me to encourage him to send it back, or did he want my assurance that since he was sensitive to the subtlety of wealth he would not be really ensnared by it?

Usually not at a loss for words, I was then because I, too, had mixed emotions about that wealth. Part of me wanted to send it back, not wanting anything to remind me of Pharoah—as he had sent everything I had touched along with me so he would not remember the unpleasantness my unwilling visit to his palace caused him. But also I thought fondly of luxuries I enjoyed and could purchase with this abundance. And there were times I thought of the hungry children we saw in other camps and in villages along our way. I knew our increased resources would let us give them more than we had in the past. At no time did I consider what God wanted done with the riches.

"I shouldn't have imposed heavy thoughts on you just now. We can talk of this another time." Abram threw back his shoulders, and I was glad to see his smile return. "Now, let's plan for the trip to Gerar tomorrow morning. We will have a wonderful holiday."

We did have happy hours in Gerar. I was glad Abram had come with me because I always enjoyed things more if I could share them with him. Lot went with us. So did Hagar and a few of the other servants.

I loved the smell of the spices and the vine-ripened fruit in the food stalls, the aroma of freshly baked bread by the bakers' ovens. My eyes drank in the delight of brightly dyed, thick-pile carpets and dramatically designed room dividers for tents. I was entranced by the heavily guarded tables laden with pieces of gleaming lapis lazuli, beryl, jacinth and amethyst. I watched the basket weavers and the artists painting designs on pottery. We walked from one merchant to another, talking and laughing as though we had not a care in the world.

Abram decided to postpone a decision about keeping our Egyptian fortune until we were back at Bethel. He would go to the altar he had built during our early days in the land. He had built many altars since then—each one a symbol of his worship of God and a sign that he was claiming this as God's land in a very special way.

Gerar had received several heavy rains before we arrived, and the trees and crops showed only slight signs of the drought of the year before. As we journeyed north it was a joy to see that things were improving all along the route. There was still some hardship in Canaan, but since the rains had begun the grazing lands were responding. Soon they would be luxuriant again, and the economy dependent on them would thrive.

Our caravan now numbered more than 500 persons and a host of animals. We had camels, donkeys, cattle and dogs. There were twelve covered oxcarts and many tents of all sizes. And we had enormous numbers of sheep and goats. Life was pleasant.

Abram brought us to a halt a short distance from Bethel. This would be our headquarters for a few months, so careful planning went into placing the tents, setting up a permanent kitchen, unpacking seldom used items and finding places for them. While Eliezer supervised all this, Abram went alone to his old altar. He remained there for many hours. Although we know our God is everywhere, He seems closer to us in some places than in others.

Apparently Abram decided to keep the wealth from Egypt. We did not mention it again.

Our herds increased, and we had so much wool to sell that it became necessary to send out small trading caravans. Zaccur was in charge of these, and we had complete confidence in his expert handling of our interests.

Lot was busy with flocks he bought in Egypt with his inheritance from Terah. He hired competent shepherds, but he kept a close eye on his investment himself and was becoming prosperous in his own right.

Abram commended him for his success. He was proud of his nephew and a bit smug at the thought that Lot had gained most of his knowledge in this business from him. He looked forward to a long, friendly rivalry but a basic cooperation between them—until the day Lot angrily approached him.

"Having two great herds in the same area can have its problems, uncle. Today I found some of my shepherds quarreling with some of your shepherds over whose animals should be watered first at the well. There has been some dissension also about the areas where each may graze their flocks. Both your shepherds and mine know their trade well and have a keen eye for the best places."

"I know, Lot. This is not a new problem, but if it is becoming more serious we must find a solution. Do you have any suggestion about the best way to handle things?"

"No."

"Let me think about it for a few days. Meanwhile, let's tell our shepherds to plan a better system to get the flocks watered and the grazing areas selected. They have a responsibility to do their job well, but that does not mean fighting about it."

Strife between the rival shepherds increased, and one of Abram's men was seriously injured when violence followed a heated argument over a watering place. Lot did not reprimand the offender, but rather attempted to justify his actions when he talked it over with Abram.

"My man was defending his right to first place at the trough for his animals. Your man started the fight, and mine was forced to respond. You said you would think this over for a few days. Have you come to any decision? Incidents such as the one today are bound to happen more often if something isn't done—and quickly."

"We will discuss it tomorrow morning right after sunup. I will meet you by the well where the trouble occurred."

I was standing in the doorway to my tent as their

conversation took place. I heard Lot's voice—petulant, insolent. Childishly, he had thrown the responsibility for the entire problem on Abram and walked away without the courtesy of saying he would meet his uncle in the morning.

Abram watched him cross the field and enter his tent. Then, with shoulders slightly drooping and his chin almost resting on his chest, he walked slowly to where I was.

"Lot no longer wants to be part of our household," Abram said. Always perceptive, he had sensed the chronic mood underlying Lot's complaints. "He is ready to be independent of us. He has proved he understands how to handle shepherds, flocks, and marketing. We must let him go. The trouble with our herdsmen is an excuse for us to separate so it will appear to be an impersonal thing. I have been aware of his uneasy restlessness for some time. I will miss him."

I wanted to run to Lot and tell him he was breaking his uncle's heart. I wanted to tell him we loved him but felt he was ungrateful after we had been like parents to him since the death of his father and Terah. Either Abram read the expression on my face or he anticipated the thoughts in my mind. He took my hand and said, "This is between Lot and me. We will work out some way to avoid bad feelings between us."

Abram went to the sacred altar and remained there until nearly dark. When he returned he said nothing about Lot, but he was calm, and his face looked untroubled.

The next morning I asked Abram if I could go with him to the meeting with Lot. I promised to be quiet the whole time. He agreed to let me come, and we both walked to the site of the well. Lot was already there.

Abram looked intently at him, then placed his hands on the young man's shoulders. "This will be your decision, Lot. Choose which section of land you want. Let's part company. If you want the land to the right, I will take the land on the left; If you want the land on the left, I will take the land on the right."

As he released Lot from the gentle embrace, we watched our nephew look thoughtfully in each direction, mentally assessing the land, the water supply, the cities with the best markets. Each of us knew which was the better choice, but the question was whether Lot would take the better land for himself, or leave the better for Abram.

"I will take the well-watered plain of Jordan." Lot's eyes narrowed as he scanned it all again. "This land reminds me of where we stayed in Egypt. It must be as beautiful as the place you have described so often at the campfires, the place of the original garden of God. There are many cities near the plain to provide good markets. I shall be very happy there."

Lot's blatant greed surprised, hurt, and infuriated me! Abram, to whom God has assigned the entire land of Canaan, would be content with the leavings of an arrogant nephew. I had promised to remain silent so I ran from the well site back to my tent lest I break that promise.

Abram did not come back to the camp until nearly dark. I made supper for him and was glad to see that he welcomed the food. When his meal was over, he talked about Lot and the division of the land.

"The part left for me to work in is more than ample for my needs. We both could have stayed here in what I have left and prospered.

"What I have been aware of for quite a while, but have been unable to change, is the basic disagreement between Lot and me about how life should be lived and what values are most important. Without going into detail about the many stormy discussions we have had, Sarai, I will tell you only that Lot plans to make his headquarters near the city of Sodom."

"No! It can't be! Everyone in Canaan knows Sodom is wicked, depraved. The mention of its name is the mention of a polluting stench!"

"We have taught him right values and he knows to fear

and worship the one God. I have told him we will welcome visits from him and have asked him to send us word of how he is getting along. We can do no more."

"This is the part which hurts most," I said, and my tears attested to that hurt. "We can do no more than watch this one, who is like a son to us, turn his back and walk away into influences we so oppose. Do you think we will see him again?"

"Of course we will. Don't be sad. Leaving home to start out independently is a normal thing. Let's not think of it as tragic."

Abram was attempting to cheer himself as well as me with his brave words. In both our hearts there was a heaviness that comes with finality. We had felt something like this when Terah died. Although the death of a parent and the breaking away of a loved one are normal processes of life, they are both heartaches. We had come to the end of another era. I knew we never would see Lot again. As it turned out, Abram did see him one more time.

It had been a difficult day, but it was ending. We were released to our own thoughts in the darkness and the stillness of the welcome night.

We awoke, refreshed by the night's rest, to a beautiful morning. Abram was standing by the door of the tent when I opened my eyes. He was looking in the direction of the road. Then he turned to me with a look of great excitement and joy. I thought that Lot had come back.

"Sarai, finally, we are in the situation to which God called me back in Ur! We are separated from all our family now. For whatever reasons I clung to the older and the younger generations, it was never God's instruction to me.

"And now, although I did not bring it to pass, it has happened. Separated from all my family, I will draw closer to God. I will go today to the altar and will stay there before Him. Oh, I long to have Him make Himself known to me again! It has been a very long time since I felt His presence as

I did when we first entered the land at the Oak of Moreh."

Abram's waiting on the Lord that day was rewarded. He came back in the evening with words that made us both affirm that our life was not ending with Lot's departure, but rather it was beginning on a higher level. God did appear to Abram again and spoke. His message this day, as His earlier messages, had been imprinted into Abram's consciousness so firmly that he had not the slightest difficulty remembering each precious word. I listened to Abram's repeating of them and shared his awed delight.

> Lift up your eyes from where you are and look north and south, east and west. All the land that you see I will give to you and your offspring forever. I will make your offspring like the dust of the earth, so that if anyone could count the dust, then your offspring could be counted. Go, walk through the length and breadth of the land, for I am giving it to you.

Part Two

Separated unto God

12

Go, walk through the length and breadth of the land, for I am giving
it to you.   *Genesis 13:17*

*S*eparated from country, people, and our father's household and renewed by God's presence, we knew it was time—God's time—to move our tents again.

Before breaking camp Abram made a trip to neighboring camps to purchase quality animals to add to our own herds. He went into Bethel and Ai to hire additional shepherds.

He spent much time talking with people he hired, instructing them about our particular way of life and the God we worship. He now allowed no one in our company to openly worship Baal or any other idol, even if the person did not actually worship the one God. One of his highest joys was seeing his shepherds and servants turn, however weakly at first, from idol worship to faith in the one God.

I tried to speak of God to Hagar several times, but she was disinterested and gave no intimation of the slightest desire to forsake the gods of Egypt, which I supposed she worshiped in private. She found companionship among the other servants who had been joined to us in Egypt, and since I had little need for a personal maid now, I saw her infrequently. When I was with her, I felt strangely uncomfortable, and I overreacted by being more exacting of her than I was of the other servants.

While Abram saw to acquiring additional servants and animals, I spent time going to various tents where our maidservants worked, checking to see if all would be ready for another series of moves.

I went first to visit the spinners, busily changing the long top fleece of goats into sturdy yarn, trying to finish an order given them by the weavers before time to close this camp. They would have little time to work in the days ahead as tents would be moved almost daily on caravan.

The skillful weavers were at their looms, weaving wide strips of very dark brown, weather-resistant cloth to be sewn together later into a fine new tent—a large one for Abram and me. These women were artisans who took pride in their work, as much in working with this drab material as when they wove colorfully dyed wool for the mats, rugs and room dividers inside the tents. Lael, still the most expert of them all, supervised their work and trained the young girls in the art.

When the little children were not playing in the fields, they took turns using woven straw fans to cool the workers.

The tent where food was stored and prepared was an enticing place. Most of the family units did their own cooking, but some of our meals—all of Eliezer's and Hagar's meals and those of others with no family cooks—were prepared here and taken to the individual tents to be eaten.

Nika, a maidservant Abram hired at Gerar, and two other women were sitting at the doorway of the kitchen tent. Each was contentedly pushing a stone back and forth in another concave stone which held grain. They would keep at this until enough meal was prepared for the day's needs. This is one job I never offered to help with, for it looked endlessly monotonous. These women countered boredom with small talk and exchanges of gossip.

There was an abundance of food inside the tent. For anyone who missed a meal for some reason there was always something available. It was beautiful. Large wicker baskets held melons, pomegranates, cucumbers and leeks. Earthenware jars held wild honey and cheese. There were containers of bread and bowls of fresh and dried grapes.

And, as a perfect garnish, in season, there would be cress and parsley.

Staples such as flour and salt were stored in tall jars or in hollow rams' horns. Dozens of animal skins were kept filled with water, milk, wine, and oil.

Occasionally, especially when a sheik came to visit Abram, meat would be roasted here. When we camped near lakes or streams, fresh fish were added to our diet, and when we were away from the water, we often ate dried fish.

Some of the store of bowls had been set out for packing. The bowls were of several sizes, most large enough to be shared by several people.

Near the bowls were long-handled copper and bronze cooking knives and ladles. When they were polished, they looked like ornaments. Those of us who used them kept personal eating utensils in our own tents, but most of the people ate with their hands or used a piece of bread to dip into the food and eat from it.

An extra supply of lamps, small clay dishes with a rim, also were kept in this tent, along with a supply of flax and hemp wicks. These already had been packed away.

Satisfied with all I had seen, I walked back toward my tent, remembering when our group had been much smaller and I had helped with the washing, cooking, and other duties. Even then the women probably had not needed my help as much as I had needed their company.

I attended women giving birth less frequently now, although I still often administered medicines and herbs to women and children who were ill. Aside from that, I kept to myself. Any spinning or weaving I did was done in my own tent. The withdrawal from other women had been unintentional and gradual, but it had become my way of life.

Moving after being in one place for a while always made me sentimental. Would I ever get used to moving? I wondered if Hagar and the other Egyptian servants were homesick.

I decided to call Hagar to wash and braid my hair before we began our trip.

Major packing began exactly on the schedule Abram set. We moved out on a cloudless morning, going with the reassurance from God that this land was ours and would be our descendants' land forever. Our descendants, longed for and already loved, were yet to be given; the land was yet to be actually possessed.

Abram and I, conscious of being far past the normal years of child bearing, encouraged ourselves by remembering other men and women we had heard of who were almost as old as we were and had been blessed with children. Our having an heir was, however, becoming more and more a challenge to our faith. God planned it should be.

As for the land of Canaan belonging to us and to our descendants forever, we considered this with some amazement because in all our travels we saw walled, fortified cities and even zealously guarded wells in the outlying countryside. Canaan looked more like an armed camp than a prize for the taking. We never contemplated leading an army to secure it by force, but trusted God to deal with the Canaanites and with their gods who encouraged them to live in depravity and violence.

This was a journey to enjoy. We moved at a leisurely pace and looked at everything with an elated sense of ownership.

We were learning two important lessons. First, God's timing and our timing were on a different scale. As children, we thought a promise meant "Now." As we grew in faith, we realized a promise could involve "Wait." The second thing we were realizing was that we must accept God's promise as substance before it became reality. All He decreed would come to pass, and in His sight it was as good as done! The mysteries of it all compounded our excitement.

Much of beautiful Canaan was familiar to us, for we had

seen it as we first came into the land and traveled from the northern part down to Gerar and the Negev. We had again seen much of it when we came back from Egypt and journeyed again to Bethel. On those trips we stayed primarily in the central highlands, but now we took side excursions from several encampments, going into Byblos, Sidon, Tyre, and Joppa, walking in the sand dunes along the great sea.

In all our travels we found much to talk about. Abram knew the present facts and the history of the places, and he spoke of them in detail. I had an alert eye for some special view of a mountain or an unusual wayside flower and called his attention to these. Together we shared Canaan — our land!

Now we were going back toward the southern part of the highlands, to Hebron. We did not plan to live in the city but would stay in the camp with our servants. Abram arranged a place for us in the gently rolling fields of Mamre, famous for its gigantic oak groves.

The tents were set up quickly, skillfully. I watched with almost as much interest as the first time I had seen it done. This time they were putting up our new tent which had been finished during our journey. The men laid the material on the ground, then crawled underneath it with 6-foot and 10-foot tent poles. They put the heads of the poles into sockets in the roof section, then raised them and pushed the ends into the ground. Next, long ropes were drawn through wooden hooks fastened on the edge of the tent roof and tied to pegs which others had pounded into the ground while the tent was being raised.

Our new tent had three large rooms. One room was mine, one was Abram's, and the other was for entertaining guests and for family meals. The new rugs, mats, cushions, and room dividers were brought in, along with other personal things. We were home.

At Mamre there were plentiful grasslands so shepherds

could take their flocks to places far enough from each other to avoid disputes over wells and borderlines.

Our shepherds had a difficult life. They were away from their homes for long weeks at a time, caring for animals that became ill, seeking any that strayed, and at times defending them against wild animals such as prowling wolves, jackals, bears, and an occasional lion which would wander in from the woods along the Jordan. Thieves were a common menace and sometimes a deadly one. The shepherds trained their dogs more for protection than for herding sheep. Abram liked to visit the different pasture areas, and I was glad when he returned safely, thankful he did not have to stay out as the shepherds did.

Overall, our life had a serenity about it in those first years there. Even the shepherds' difficulties had been fewer than at other places. There were no pressing problems, no special needs. Our God knew we needed rest after the upheaval of the famine, the trip into Egypt and back, our separation from Lot—even from the thrilling but strenuous walking through the land.

Abram built a large altar from native stone—uncut, unpolished—to our God.

13

Blessed be Abram by God Most High,
Creator of heaven and earth.
And blessed be God Most High,
who delivered your enemies into your hand.
Genesis 14:19-20

*T*he placid tranquility of Mamre ended abruptly. It happened on a day Abram and Zaccur took wool into Hebron to sell. Abram had always enjoyed these trips, and they had become even more interesting for him since he had met Ephron, wealthiest landowner in Hebron. The two men had become friends and enjoyed long conversations after business hours were over. Abram usually came home with interesting news and in a very good humor. This time, as I watched him get down from his mount and walk toward our tent, he looked preoccupied with serious thoughts. He came in without speaking.

After a few minutes I asked, "Did the day go well? Was there a good price for the wool?"

"What did you say?"

"I asked how the day went for you and if the market was good."

"The wool is sold and at a fine price."

I put supper on the table mat for him. He ate it without comment, then became restless and walked out into the yard around our tent. He paced back and forth for a while to work out tensions, and when he came back in he looked calmer.

"There is disturbing news today. It involves Lot. There

was a man from Sodom at the marketplace today who said his city and neighboring cities are preparing for an attack by King Kedorlaomer of Elam and other kings allied with him. Kedorlaomer's forces subdued these cities nearly fourteen years ago and required them to pay heavy tribute. Just recently the rulers of these cities got together and decided to refuse to continue the excessive payments: They thought they were getting away with their rebellion since they heard no immediate reaction to their daring. But now they have learned they are under threat of imminent attack. Kedorlaomer, along with Amraphel king of Shinar, Arioch king of Ellaser, and Tidal king of other cities are on their way to do battle. They are barbaric and merciless, totally destroying cities and whole populations in other places where they have been defied."

In his characteristic way, Abram had catalogued as many facts about the situation as he could. I heard little of what he said except what mattered to me—Lot's situation.

"Abram, do you think Lot does not know about this? Won't he quickly move his camp to a safer place?"

"I haven't told you before but now you must know. Lot is no longer a herdsman; he sold all of his animals and dismissed his shepherds some months ago. He married a woman of Sodom and lives in a house he bought there. He is a merchant and a friend of those involved in the city administration."

I made no comment, waiting for Abram to continue.

"King Bera of Sodom will be the leader of the bold front against the aggressor from the north. Birsha king of Gomorrah, Shinab king of Admah, and Shemeber king of Zeboiim will stand with him to face their common enemy."

"Can we get word to Lot—and his wife—to come to stay with us until this is over? Is there time?

"I have thought of that, but Lot must choose his own battles. He has always had our invitation to return at any time to our camp. He has never come, nor has he sent any messages. If he comes now as a refugee, we will take him in. But I doubt he will come, especially if he is in need—call it foolish pride, or courage."

Abram sent a messenger to Hebron every day to pick up further word from Sodom or its allies. News was scarce because no one was allowed to leave the cities which were readying for the onslaught.

Then came the day our messenger returned from Hebron with a wounded man who was weak from terror and from the exertion of a painful, slow, furtive walk from Sodom to Hebron. At first we did not recognize him but suddenly Abram cried, "Joram! Joram, what has happened to you?"

I remembered Joram well. He was Lot's chief shepherd— and troublemaker—while we were all at Bethel. I listened intently as he laboriously tried to answer Abram's questions.

"Wounded...battle...Kedorlaomer..." With those three words, loaded heavily with tragedy, he slumped into unconsciousness.

Abram had him taken to a tent where his head wounds were tended, and the deep slash in his left arm was cleansed and bandaged. A guard stayed at his bedside to minister further to him, applying cool wet towels to his fevered body and, when possible, attempting to get him to drink some water.

While we waited for him to regain consciousness, we imagined every possible thing he might tell us about Lot. After several hours he rallied enough to call for Abram and tried to explain what had occurred. Abram told me about it later.

"Joram spoke in snatches of sentences, but his message was clear. The clash came in the Valley of Siddim by the Salt Sea. The five rebel kings led their men out to stop the four attacking kings. The battle became a rout as the forces of the defenders were overwhelmed by their ferocious old enemies. The kings of both Sodom and Gomorrah fled into hiding. The leaderless, confused men ran in total disarray. Many deserted to the hills. Others futilely attempted to dodge the spears and lances. Some were forced into the sea. The invading kings seized all the goods of Sodom and Gomorrah, even their stores of food.

They took many prisoners, Sarai."

"Including Lot?" I knew the answer from Abram's face.

"Including Lot, his wife, and all their possessions."

Abram turned and strode swiftly from our tent. I knew what he was going to do. As father Terah had done before him, Abram always kept a company of well-trained guards who could be ready in moments to meet any violence that might threaten our camp. He immediately called them together and told them to get ready to march, and he asked each one to take along another of the servants who could help fight. Then he went to the altar in the oak grove.

He came back to the tent and took from its place a curved shield, a leather helmet and a sword.

"Abram," a strained voice I hardly recognized as my own said, "you have never been in battle before!"

He smiled a little sadly as he replied, "Everyone who battles goes once for the first time. And, Sarai, my hope of victory is not in my own bravery or military skill, nor is it in the abilities of these fine young men, drilled only in the mere basics of warfare. My hope is in the strength God will give us as we chase these kings from the land and rescue all they are taking with them as spoils of battle."

"Are you afraid at all?"

He took my hand and stood as if taking inventory of his feelings. Then he said, "Remember how we talked about doubts and fears not excluding faith, but only challenging it? Yes, I am afraid. And that means since I cannot rely on myself, I must trust God even more. I go in some fear, but I go in great faith."

To my valiant warrior—a totally new facet of my beloved husband's character—I answered, "And I fear to have you go, but will allow this to be a reason for my own faith to increase. God, who has promised us the land, will bring you back safely," I managed to smile, "for our descendants' sake."

With those moments of mutual encouragement he went out to meet his men at the drill field for a final briefing. I followed at a distance, as did the wives, mothers and fathers of the other men who would be going.

There were 318 men in Abram's small army. Each one had the implement he could handle best—lance, bow and arrows, battle axe, saw-toothed dagger, spear, sword, mace, even slingshot. The regular guards had leather helmets and shields. The others improvised protective covering using animal skins or whatever material they could find. Abram took his place at the head of the columns that had formed. We watched them go, each carrying his weapon, a pouch with bread, and a skin of water. Abram began one of the songs they sang at the campfires, and the men joined in. So did those left behind.

Work schedules in the camp were drastically rearranged. The older men took the places of the herdsmen. The women and children worked in the gardens and fields. For all of us, these were days of waiting and eager watching for any sign of the men's return—days of fears and hopes and prayers.

Everyday tasks began to be neglected, not because we were lazy, but because with our loved ones away in combat, our work lost its importance.

Eliezer assumed leadership in Abram's absence. He was our faithful servant, a man of faith beloved by Abram and me. One evening he arranged for a special campfire and urged everyone to gather around it. He spoke to us in a voice ringing with confidence. His words were carefully chosen to encourage us to be at our best. "When our master returns, we want him to be as pleased with the way we have kept things here as he will be pleased with the way our fighting men have won their victory!"

Those were wise words, and we found that hard,

productive work, keeping the camp and flocks in good order, helped us pass the time more easily. It also made the return of the men more real in our own minds.

More than two weeks later a guard who was posted on the road into Hebron raced back to camp, screaming the news as he came, "They are coming! They are here!"

Our men were home! All 318 were safe, and their faces were shining with the joy of victory. There was laughing, talking, warm embracing. The children clapped hands and literally danced with delight.

All this noisy jubilee was a background for my own enraptured moment of knowing Abram was with me again, well and strong, pressed close to my heart.

After the surge of private greetings began to ebb, Abram raised his arms and called for quiet. He was a man who could command attention readily, even at a joyfully wild time like this.

"No work but the most necessary for three days, then we will have a great feast of celebration. Now I will go to the altar of our God and present a sacrifice of praise to Him for bringing us this marvelous victory."

Abram had no taste for relating the gruesome details of war. He told me just enough to get a general idea of what had happened.

Abram and his men covertly pursued the enemy all the way to Dan, then attacked the battle-weary armies, taking them by total surprise. The soldiers who survived their attack retreated swiftly, using the prisoners now as hostages. Abram's army went after them, and finally at Hobah, north of Damascus, there was a confrontation. The enemy surrendered completely, giving up the loot they had taken and all their prisoners.

About his meeting with Lot he said only that it was a warm, tearful reunion followed by an awkward silence.

I had wanted to press for more details about Lot. Was

there a chance he might not return to Sodom? Would he possibly come to us now? I left the questions unasked when I saw how painful the subject of our nephew had become to him. Abram was safely home from a victorious war, but he had suffered a personal heartbreak.

He stopped speaking of the battles and of Lot. He leaned back and looked out the doorway of our tent as if trying to gain composure from the sight of the massive oak trees, the sky, and the peaceful camp. I thought his conversation with me had ended, but as I started to go into my own room, he motioned for me to stay.

"Sarai, I had to tell you about the battle and about Lot first because I wanted to settle your mind about them. You know as much as you need to know about all that now. When you are ready for more news, I will tell you what else happened. I have saved the telling of this until last because it is most special, and I didn't want to mix it with the rush of words over the other matters."

"If there is more, I want to hear it right away!"

"Part of it will be as difficult to explain as the times when God speaks to me. I met a man who . . . . I will come back to that later.

"As I was returning with my men, the released prisoners, and their possessions, the king of Sodom met me in the Valley of Shaveh. He had come out of his hiding place when he knew he would be safe and had sent scouts to learn what happened after the kings left on their triumphant march back to their home cities. He had been delighted to learn of the defeat we had dealt them, and he kept informed all the time of our progress in bringing the people and the goods back to their homes.

"He came out to meet us with great pomp. There was a display of all the regal trappings he could find. There were musicians, dancing girls, and tables of food he had managed to bring out from somewhere. He had prepared a speech and had just begun to deliver it when a tall, white-haired man walked authoritatively to a place beside King Bera. He seemed not to see the king at all but looked steadily at me.

"This great man held in his hands a loaf of bread and a container of wine which he offered me.

"There was not a sound from anywhere in the Valley of Shaveh. This is a contradiction of terms, but Sarai, it was a silence you could hear!

"I accepted the bread and the wine and, as he indicated I should, I ate and drank of them."

Abram did not speak then for a brief time. He seemed about to start several times but would stop short of actually saying anything. He shook his head, impatient with himself, then relaxed into a bit of a smile and continued, "Whenever I think of words to describe this man, I find them inadequate. But listen with your heart, Sarai, and I will try.

"There was a quality of light about him, and he was the essence of strength. He evoked intense excitement from those around him, but he himself was the personification of peace. There was a blessed joy that shined in his eyes, and he smiled easily, a wonderfully warm, encouraging smile.

"'I am Melchizedek,' he said. When I describe the sound of his voice, it will be as weak a description as the attempt to tell you how he looked—but, again I will try. Imagine softness, cadence and drama perfectly blended.

"That incomparable voice said, 'I am King of Salem, the priest of El Elyon, God Most High.'

"I felt an immediate response like some kind of inner flame leaping through my total being. In astonishment I stood in the presence of the priest of God Most High—the priest of my God! El Elyon had sent His priest to minister to me. Sarai, he called me by name!

"And he said, 'I have a blessing for you, Abram.' He took back the remaining bread and wine and gave them to one of his servants to replace in the basket from which he had taken them. The sun seemed to shine more radiantly, and I felt a soft, refreshing breeze as he put his hand on my head, saying,

    'Blessed be Abram by God Most High,

    Creator of heaven and earth.

    And blessed be God Most High

    Who delivered your enemies into your hand.'

"I have said those words over and over. I have even sung them, Sarai! Blessed be God Most High!"

Abram had made the scene live again in his own mind, as he had caused it to live in mine. We shared a quiet like the stillness he described in the Valley of Shaveh when Melchizedek appeared. We each had our own thoughts of wonder, love, and praise, our own joyful tears.

Abram broke the silence, calling us both back from the captivating reverie. "I gave him an offering of one-tenth of all the spoils of our battle. He accepted the offering in the powerful name of El Elyon, then went with his aides back to the road leading to Salem, near Mt. Moriah.

"King Bera, paled by what had just happened and obviously relieved that the king of Salem had left, took charge of things again and made a magnanimous offer to me: 'Give me the people and keep the goods for yourself.'"

My mind reeled at the thought of the amount of treasure this would be. "He was giving you all the possessions of all the people you had rescued?"

"Yes. Bera found it easy to be generous with other people's possessions!"

"That would be fortunes and fortunes! Did you accept it?"

"Nothing Bera could have given me would have meant anything at all after being blessed by the priest of God Most High. Bera offered trinkets. I know Melchizedek came to me just before this great offer of unimaginable wealth so I would not be tempted to accept it, as I had once accepted a much lesser gift from Pharaoh. God Most High gave me the victory in two battles—the physical one and the spiritual one.

"I did accept reimbursement for our expenses and a suitable portion for my men. But for myself I took nothing. I would not have the king of Sodom brag about being my benefactor and think he had any reason to take credit for my prosperity. I want no alliance with him and no obligation to him.

"Sarai, you would have liked my last remark to Bera. I told him I would not take a thread or even the thong of a sandal for myself!"

I laughed in delighted surprise at Abram's sense of humor coming to the surface in so serious a moment. Then I laughed in wonder at myself, realizing I didn't want all those possessions either. God Most High was freeing both of us from our desire for more and more things, and the freedom was fine!

"Did you really say that to King Bera? I would like to have heard you, and I would like to have seen the look on his face. I am glad you told him exactly what you did. Who needs sandal thongs or anything? We have all we need. We have everything!"

As I said those brave, happy words a chilling inner voice in my head said, "Not everything. You do not have a child!" Was it my untrusting self that spoke, or was it an evil spirit trying to undermine my joy at having Abram safely home from war, victor in battle and in temptation—and blessed by God? Whatever the source, my gladness was not dimmed, and with Abram's strong arms around me I thanked our God for such a husband as he.

Abram had walked through the land in peace and in war.

14

...and he was called God's friend.   *James 2:23*

 *A*fter I told Ephron about the battle and how we chased Kedorlaomer and his armies all the way to Hobah with our small army, I told him no such thing would have been possible if God Most High had not been for us!" Abram had just returned from a visit with Ephron and, of course, had told in detail the account of the recent victory.

"Was Ephron impressed?"

"Yes. Enough to give me the ultimate compliment of my life."

"That you are bravest of all?"

"No."

"That you are the wisest strategist?"

"No!"

"That you are the best story teller?" I could not resist my habit of teasing Abram. He was always patient with my attempts to keep him from being too serious.

"Sarai," he said, so softly that I had to listen well to hear him, "Ephron said if I won the battle that decisively, with the odds that were against me, God most certainly was with me. He even gave me a new name."

"What name did Ephron give you?" I asked in wonder, for I could not imagine any name that could cause Abram's face to be so flushed with the quiet excitement he obviously was savoring.

He cleared his throat so he could speak more easily. "Ephron said he would call me 'Friend of God.'"

"That is a title to be proud of, a challenge to live up to."

"Yes, and it is a name that humbles me, reminding me
that He chose me. I don't know why He did. I was a nobody
who thought he was somebody in Ur. But I know He chose
me, and I worship this most high and holy God. I want to be
His man insofar as I am able, but I never thought of the
concept of being His friend until Ephron mentioned it. At
first it seemed an effrontery — friend of God! Worshiper of
God, yes! Servant of God, yes! But, friend of God? The idea
seemed presumptuous when he first suggested it. But now I
think God Himself caused old Ephron to call me that just to
draw me closer to Himself. There is amazing mystery in it
all — my meeting God as friend with Friend! I understand it
though, for I have been conscious of a growing gladness as I
anticipate each meeting with Him. The old, awesome fear is
being sweetened through blessed communion with God
Most High."

The next morning Abram ate a hurried breakfast. Then
he said, "I am going to see Neri out in the field and ask him
to select the most perfect male lamb from the flocks and take
it to the altar for me. I will sacrifice it to my Friend, and I will
stay there in fellowship with Him for the rest of the day."

As he walked out of the tent to begin his day's activities
I thought of the battle and how it had deepened the relationship between the Lord God and Abram. I knew this account
would be added to the sacred traditions and passed down
from generation to generation. No one would be able to tell
it with more style and exuberance than Abram, and I looked
forward to hearing it many times around our campfires.
With each telling I knew I would feel the same joy and pride
in him and in the men who went with him — and in those
who stayed home battling fears and tensions while keeping
things in order.

Since this was a very special time for my husband, I
decided to make it more festive by having some cakes ready

when he came back for supper. Baking took much time so I
began early. I had two earthenware containers. One was for
barley flour used for daily bread, and one was for wheat
flour used for fancy bread and cakes. Today called for wheat
flour. I measured out enough, and, although Nika had
ground it with the stones, it was not fine enough for cakes. I
ground it further with mortar and pestle. When it looked
right, I added salt and kneaded it with honey and oil, finally
pressing it into flat loaves. This procedure, so familiar to me,
was pleasant. I liked the texture of the dough as I worked it,
and I liked the fragile fragrance of the honey. When the
cakes were ready to bake, I took them to the oven tended by
Nika and her helpers. Sometimes I waited while the cakes
baked, turning them so they would not burn and so they
would be well done on both sides. Today I asked Nika to do
it for me, because I had other work to do and could not take
time to watch them.

"Bring them to my tent when they are baked, Nika."

"I will. Do you need anything else?"

"After today's baking my wheat flour is nearly gone. You
can send some one with a new supply in a day or so. Thank
you, Nika."

And as I walked back to my tent, I thought to thank
Another. "Thank You for the bountiful supply of flour.
Never again will I take it for granted, since I have known
famine. Thank You for the gentle rains that make the grain
grow and the sunshine that ripens it into golden stalks which
bend beneath caressing breezes. Thank You for the strength
of the men and women who harvest it, separating grain from
chaff. Thank You for the life-sustaining bread made from
the grain. And now a special torrent of gratitude, O God
Most High, overwhelms me as I think of the cakes that are
baking in our oven. May they be eaten in celebration and in
praise this evening in our tent."

I hummed one of our campfire songs as I got things ready
to finish the piece of cloth I was weaving. It was fine linen of

pale blue and was to be made into a tunic for Abram. I worked on it while he was away, for it was to be a surprise. After the tunic was finished, I planned to weave linen for a turban and sash to complete the elegant outfit. Abram would look so grand!

My mind worked ahead of what my hands could do, and as I wove the blue cloth, I was planning a soft wool blanket, using yellow and brown yarns. My days were busy and I liked them that way.

Sometimes I was interrupted in my weaving, embroidery, or cooking to go to the tent of one who was ill. Early in our days of caravan Abram had taught me about herbs and other medications. I had picked up additional knowledge of such things from women in our own and neighboring camps through the years. I worked with ingredients from commonplace things—roots, bark, and leaves of trees; bitter-tasting gum resins; herbs like thyme and mustard; oil from castor beans; extract of pomegranate root; sea onion juice; and olive oil. To be used with caution were the seeds of the poppy plant and a rare root from the east that I gave when other medicines did not help. It was exciting, being able to comfort some one, or actually to effect a cure. I added loving care to the ointments being applied and offered encouragement along with the medicines being given. To see a child run and play again was a joy. To see a mother restored to health and able to care for her family again had been rewarding for me many times.

My caring for the women and children gave me a very affectionate feeling for them. Some of the babies I had helped deliver back at Haran and even later seemed to be "my babies," and my love for them continued long after the birthing process. I watched them grow with fond interest. Many of "my boys" were with Abram when he went against Kedorlaomer.

After we returned from Egypt, our group was so large that we needed other midwives for the many babies born to our women. Also, I gradually stopped helping at births, except when necessary, because of a serious complication. There had grown within me a hurting jealousy when I saw the mother, exhausted by labor but filled with ecstasy, feel the warm little body of the child I placed in her arms, count tiny toes and fingers, and beam with pride at her baby's first lusty cries. Baking, weaving, and embroidering were not as emotionally trying, and I turned to them as a refuge.

Nika herself brought the baked cakes, not entrusting them to anyone else. She had given them careful attention, and they had browned beautifully. They were still warm, and their fragrance was tantalizing. They would taste best right now.

"Nika, let's have a small piece of one of these cakes. Can you stay to have some with me?"

Her smile and nod of assent were quick. I broke off a piece for her and one for me, and we relaxed into a time of good conversation.

She often was a source of information for me, and I could learn from her of major problems or joys among our people. Today the news concentrated on how happy everyone was that the time of battle was over and how honored Abram was among them for his leadership. She said many women had brought wheat cakes to the oven for baking that day. The three-day celebration, ending with the great feast Abram had ordered, was over, and yet the people continued to fete their own personal heroes privately.

I would have liked for our conversation to go on, but it was getting late, and I drew it to a close. "God's blessing is over us like a canopy, Nika. Bless God Most High!"

Our impromptu party ended. After a spontaneous embrace Nika went back to her work, and I resumed mine. My immediate task was to put the loom away and begin the evening meal before Abram came back.

Supper time, it turned out, was later than usual. After his

time of waiting before the Lord God at the altar, Abram had gone to different pasture areas, talking with the shepherds about their flocks and how they felt since returning to such quiet work after the excitement of warfare.

"Sarai, our having gone to battle seems to have made the men more grateful for our place of peace here at Mamre. They know of skirmishes between clans and between cities from time to time, and they are thankful, as I am, that we have been called into this kind of thing only once—and that all 318 came back safely!

"I encouraged them to be thankful—always—and to give their thanks to the one God. And Sarai, several of them told me they had gone to the altar I built and gave their own thanksgiving to Him. Three of them even sacrificed a lamb from their flock and made full restitution for its cost to Neri."

As I cleared away the supper things, I told him of my talk with Nika and her report that the mood of the women was equally happy. They were, in fact, still celebrating. Several of them had made cakes for their men for supper as I had done.

"Their cakes will not be as delicious as the ones you made. I don't know what it is you do to make them unique, but I never tasted cake that is quite like yours."

"It's my secret," I answered, affecting a mock air of mystery. Actually there was nothing special in them at all, but it pleased me to have Abram think so.

We walked out of the tent, and I looked at our widespread, quiet camp. He went back inside and returned with a thick rug, spread it on the ground, and, taking my hand, pulled me down beside him to sit and look at the stars and watch the moon just coming over the wooded hill on the far side of our encampment.

For a while we said nothing, needing no spoken words. We sat there just holding hands and sharing the beauty of the night and the glory in our hearts.

"At times like this", Abram began, "I wonder if we will feel discouraged or sad, ever again."

"Most probably we will, and then we will wonder if we ever will feel glad again. It seems God leaves me when I am sad."

"Sarai, we must both come to trust God so completely that circumstances cannot keep us from feeling His presence—as we know it this night. I don't mean we ever would find battle as welcome as sitting under the moonlit skies. I don't mean we ever would think it fun to be ill. We may often be frustrated in little things. But if these things take away our joy in our God and make us think He is far from us, then we still depend on circumstances and not on God."

"I don't know if I ever want to reach that high level of trust you are talking about. I would rather have circumstances pleasant than be such a giant of faith that pleasant circumstances were no longer important to me. Is that wrong?"

Abram didn't answer. I waited a few minutes and answered myself. "It sounds wrong. It at least sounds childish. If I ever do come to a faith like that—not dependent on having what I want so much—it will be because God just gives me all that faith as a gift. It is not in me to be so noble, although I wish it were."

"Sarai, I believe that as we reach each plateau in our friendship with God Most High, He will encourage us to go to a higher one. I believe the climbing will continue to be difficult even though He helps us. But when we have climbed, He will let us share greater and greater views from those newly gained heights. It will no longer be like looking at snow-topped Mt. Hermon from the almond-tree-covered slopes of its foothills. It will be like standing on Mt. Hermon itself and enjoying the fine composite of groves, fields, flowers, hills, and glistening, splashing waterfalls rushing to the beautiful Kinnereth!"

"I suppose that is right, but, Abram, I hope we are nearly at the top of your symbolic mountain, for I am not such an eager climber. We must be nearly there. At least God has given us a beautiful vista tonight — both the real heavens and the joy inside us that accentuates their beauty."

It was a night too exquisite to leave. We stayed outside until nearly daybreak, watching the moon rise higher in the skies, flooding the fields with soft light and absorbing the stars in its mellow glow.

The following weeks were busy ones for Abram. He and Eliezer outfitted a trading caravan for Zaccur to lead to the Damascus bazaars. The major items were excellent wool and well-designed, expertly woven blankets. He also talked with different shepherds about their flocks and spent several days with Neri planning for the increase and distribution of flocks in the coming year. He scarcely had time to go into Hebron for his weekly visit with Ephron.

I was busy also, finishing the linen outfit for Abram, doing the bread baking and making an occasional cake. I also found time to invite other special maidservants to my tent for conversation, and twice Ephron's wife visited me. I had Hagar come occasionally to wash my hair and polish my nails. We were finding it easier to be comfortable in each other's presence as time separated us further and further from the emotionally charged days we spent together in Egypt. I tried to think more objectively of her, and she was carrying out her promise to serve me well. It seemed we were both trying to come to a measure of that friendship I had hoped we would have when I realized she would become part of our household.

I noticed Abram had been growing more quiet. He often seemed tense, as if waiting for something. I thought perhaps he had been working too hard and planned to suggest he let Eliezer, Zaccur, and Neri take more responsibility.

Then one evening when we had finished supper and were

listening to Neri's familiar pipe across the field as he played well loved shepherd's tunes and made up some new ones, Abram seemed to relax more than he had for days, soothed by that faint, sweet music.

"What was that?" Abram suddenly scrambled to his feet and ran to the doorway, so frightened that he held the tent flaps for support and searched the surroundings with frightened eyes.

"I heard nothing except the music."

"Listen! There it is again!"

I still heard nothing but did not say so. After listening intently for a few minutes Abram picked up his spear and walked out into the night. I listened hard and leaned forward as if that could make me hear better, but I heard no sound except Abram's strained voice as he called out several times, "Who is there?"

He came in later, saying whatever or whoever it was had gone away. He slept fitfully that night and was gone by daybreak. I knew he would be at the altar. I hoped his Friend would appear to him, but he returned in the afternoon still tense.

There were no more dramatic outcries, but he was on guard most of the time, listening for something. He tried not to worry me with his fears but he could not hide them.

"What is troubling you, Abram?"

"Nothing. Did you see what a fine supper I ate? Could anything be troubling me when I eat like that?"

He knew I was not convinced, but I could not persuade him to tell me what was bothering him. I could not make him understand that not knowing the problem caused more anxiety than if I knew what it was we had to face.

"Sarai, there is no problem. Don't worry."

There was a problem. I worried about a problem that had no face or name. Why couldn't Abram understand that this sort of elusive foe is more difficult to fight than one you can see?

"Abram, do you think we are climbing one of those plateaus we talked about after our celebration supper?"

"Plateaus?" He slowly smiled, remembering our conversation on that treasured evening. "Quite possibly we are. It is strange how that kind of climbing can feel like being brought lower for a while."

"Would it not help to talk about what is troubling you?"

"No."

"Abram, friend of God, let yourself rest from this strain and trust your Friend to handle whatever is wrong."

He nodded that he would, closed his eyes and wiped away some tears with a work-roughened hand. In a moment he opened his eyes, and there was life and joy in them. He kissed me gently, and with his old confident smile he told me he was going to bed early because he planned for another day of waiting before his Friend.

The faith of Abram—and my faith—in El Elyon was real. Yet we experienced highs and lows of feeling in spite of our good intent. But God used both our highs and our lows. He worked through them with divine force to drive us always closer to Himself!

15

...Abram said, "O Sovereign Lord, how can I know...?"
Genesis 15:8

*S*upper had been ready for hours, and I had already eaten when Abram came back. From the look on his face I knew it would be stupid to offer him food, although he should have been ravenous by then. He was too excited to sit down or even stand still. He paced the tent, back and forth, looking all the time like someone bursting with marvelous news—too wonderful to express in words, but too splendorous to keep inside. This was his usual pattern. He hesitated to use ordinary words to tell of extraordinary things, but he always came to terms with the limits of vocabulary after an initial struggle.

This time when the words came, there was no holding them back. They streamed out in joyful, bubbling vigor. "He was there! My Friend was there! And He knew the things that were weighing on me without my even telling Him. Since those things are resolved now, Sarai, I will tell you about them. I suppose I didn't tell you before because I was ashamed of the thoughts I was having.

"I had been afraid, very much afraid, of Kedorlaomer and his armies. This man is a defeated enemy who must be chafing more and more because of the way a small army overcame him and his allies. I thought he would take immediate revenge. I kept dwelling on how vulnerable we are here in the unwalled fields of Mamre. He could swoop down on our herds and tents, applying the torch and the sword in the manner that had made him infamous! I had no illusion that Lot or Bela or anyone else, except maybe Ephron and a few others, would try to help me at all. I worried about this so much my fears became almost reality to me. Do you remember the night I thought they had come and rushed out to fight?

"My Friend knew about this fear and did not upbraid me for it. In the crystal clarity of that beloved voice there came words of reassuring love, 'Do not be afraid, Abram. I am your shield.'

"For a long while after He spoke I was quiet before Him, absorbing the wondrous, ever-new certainty that He was actually there. I drew strength from each of the precious words, saying them over one by one, asking my Friend to bring into my mind what each one fully meant. Sarai, it is a transcendent thought. He did not say, 'I was your shield in battle,' nor did He say, 'I will be your shield if there is another crisis.' He blended past, present, and future together, saying, 'I am your shield.' That is moment by moment, forever!

"There is no more awe-filled experience than to know you are in the presence of God Most High. There is no more exalted experience than to hear Him call you by name, as a friend!

"Have you guessed that I had other negative thoughts? In addition to my fear of Kedorlaomer I had a remnant of regret about the wealth I turned down when Bela offered it. I'm too good a business man to think lightly of what I missed. I wondered if it had been naive or rash not to take at least part of it. I was looking stupid in my own eyes.

"Again, He knew about my struggle, and again there was no reproach from my Lord. Instead He shared more priceless words to add to the first: 'Do not be afraid, Abram. I am your shield,—your very great reward.'

"Those words pierced like a streak of lightning. He offers not only His protection, but Himself! He was saying that He is mine! I can understand that I am His, that I belong to Him. But that He is mine—this is something to be pondered for a lifetime.

"I was first embarrassed that He knew of my fears and my lingering interest in the riches of Sodom, but His perfect understanding of me and His lack of condemnation brought me to a deeper devotion to Him than I have ever known before. Hours flew by as I stayed there praising Him and realizing the glory He wants to share with me!

"Sarai, my increased devotion cast out fear so totally that I brought myself to ask Him directly about His old, old promise of a child. I told Him that as things were now, our servant, Eliezer of Damascus, would be our only heir!"

"No! Did you really say that?" I knew if he said he asked that question, he really had—but I wanted to hear it again.

He had not heard my interruption and continued with his divinely communicated reassurance.

"The word of the Lord came, saying, 'This man will not be your heir, but a son coming from your own body will be your heir.'

"By now it was dark. He called me out of the grove of trees where I had been sitting to the top of a rise where I could see the star-filled sky. He said, 'Look up at the heavens and count the stars—if indeed you can count them. So shall your offspring be.'"

I, no longer believing we would have even one child, could not even try to comprehend the paradox of what I had just heard—descendants as numberless as the stars, but no child! I thought it sounded marvelous, but poetic—not really applying to us at all. I hated my doubts, but they were there. And now I made Abram listen to me. I was thrilled, but actually quivering with the onslaught of assorted emotions. "Abram! Please hear me now. You were there, and being there, hearing this from God Himself, would make it more understandable, I am sure. But I am having real difficuly in accepting all this, at least at the first hearing.

I don't mean to doubt you, or God, but...."

"Yes, being there.... In the intimacy of that moment when He spoke, I had no difficulty with doubts. I felt a warmth surge all through me from His energizing love.

"But then, Sarai, when that first ecstatic time had passed, my mind also became a battlefield as doubts and fears tried to come back in—that quickly! I wanted them out but couldn't release them. I knew the One who had known my mind before would know the thoughts that had come trooping back. I wanted to run, but where can you hide from our God? Not able to run, I faced Him with my questions.

"He responded, 'I am the Lord, who brought you out of Ur of the Chaldeans to give you this land to take possession of it.'"

"Did that settle your mind again?"

"Not completely. Although later when I thought more about it and considered all He has done for us since we left Ur, I knew I should have been satisfied. As it was, I found the boldness to ask what I realized He knew was in my mind. 'O Sovereign Lord, how can I know that I will gain possession of it?'"

"Oh, Abram, did He give you a sign, a tangible token? I would like that, too—something we could touch or see, especially since I have not had the blessing of hearing His voice!"

"The token will be given tomorrow. I suppose it is already tomorrow; the morning light is showing on the hills I can see from the doorway."

"What will the token be? Did He tell you?"

"Yes. It will be a ceremony of covenant between God and me. I will sleep now. Then in a few hours I will begin preparing for it."

The covenant ritual! The most binding, unbreakable contract! The rite used in business ventures of greatest importance and carrying with it a fearful solemnity because of the fate that would come to the one who ever broke it! Could Abram make such a covenant with God? Even the best of men hesitated to enter into such an agreement with each other for they know how possible it is for one to default, even unintentionally—leaving the way open for a brutal death! I knew of the ritual in a rather vague way but soon would see it take place. Would I see God, too? Hear His voice? Would He actually come to a covenant place at Mamre?

We awoke with excitement after a few hours of sleep. Eager to prepare for the contract, Abram refused breakfast even though he had not eaten supper the night before. He hurried to secure the animals needed to meet local laws regarding ceremonial contracts.

All merchants and landowners were familiar with the standard requirements: a three-year-old heifer, a three-year-old goat, a three-year-old ram, a turtledove, and a young pigeon. These were killed. The heifer, goat, and ram were cut in half. One part of each animal was put on one side of a path, the other part on the opposite side. The birds were not dissected. The two persons making the contract would walk between the sundered animals with the understanding they were willing to accept such a fate if they ever broke the contract.

I walked out to the field where it was to take place and watched as Abram accepted the slain animals from Neri. He cut the animals in two. The sight, which did repel me, was secondary to the horrifying thought that Abram was staking his life on his ability to maintain his part of a covenant with God Most High! As much as I loved and admired him, as much as I felt he was a man of faith who put his faith into action, I wondered if he could keep—always—every point of the contract. If not, the result would be a working out of the contract's terrible terms of forfeiture.

Thinking of the grisly details of the covenant ritual, I fervently wished it had not been necessary. As I recoiled from it, I ached with deep remorse that our faith had been so unsteady that our God had to provide a visible covenant with His friend.

Everything was ready now. How would our God appear? When would He appear? My heart was racing, and as He delayed, my excitement grew. Some of our servants, having heard of the anticipated event, stood nearby. I welcomed their interest — and their company. Vigils always have been difficult for me, and tensions are eased if others are around.

By the time the sun was directly overhead, we were still watching. Excitement had ebbed. We were hot and tired. An attitude of disinterest was evidenced in the servants, and I suppose in me also. We could no longer maintain our high level of expectancy. Some of the servants eased away, preferring to go back to their duties rather than stand in the sun to watch an old man wait for his God. I was embarrassed for Abram. What had gone wrong? Had God changed His mind about coming without letting His friend know? I heard some laughter among the servants who left the field, but I was too unsure of my own emotions to risk disciplining them.

In spite of the apparent foolishness of Abram's situation he showed no sign of frustration or anxiety. Over the years he had grown accustomed to waiting long hours for his communications from God. Those hours, he told me, are not wasted but a necessary and delightful prelude of freeing oneself from thoughts and cares and freeing one's mind to high thoughts of our great God — of things He has done in past ages and in our own lives, and of things He has promised to do in the future — of just thinking about the qualities of God Himself! These were quite different thoughts from the ones I and the servants had — "how?" "how soon?" and "what if?"

Sun-filled hours had made the slain animals attractive lures to vultures. Several times Abram rushed at the birds to chase them away. He did not leave his post even for the midday meal. Eliezer took water to him but he wanted nothing more.

He looked tired but no one could wait in his place and he wanted no conversation to help pass the time. He had his own thoughts, and, judging from his face, they were glowing ones. The hours marked succeeding heights of Abram's faith!

I went back to the tent and bathed my face and arms in scented water Hagar had left in a pitcher for me. I did not want any food, but was glad to ease down on a thick mat to rest for a while. I sipped water from a painted goblet that had been a favorite even back in the house at Ur when I was a child. There was something comforting about an object that had been around so long, and the water it held was refreshing after the long session in the sun.

Toward evening I walked back to the field. Abram was still standing at the covenant site. I walked over to Eliezer who was watching from a short distance, protectively. "Has he had any food, Eliezer?"

"No. I brought some to him but he refused it. He has had only water all day."

"When you talked with him did he seem discouraged?"

"No. He knows his God will come."

"Do you think He will come, Eliezer?"

"I hope He will, and I hope I shall see Him!"

"Have you eaten today?"

"No, but I am not hungry. I will eat later, when my master does."

We saw Abram sit down, lean against a small tree and close his eyes. He seemed to be taking a well-earned nap after his long, tiring vigil.

Heavy clouds were billowing up. Although it was not time for sunset, it was almost dark. The clouds were terrifying. I wanted all three of us to get back to our tents. The wind was getting stronger, and the darkness more ominous.

"Do you think we can persuade him to leave this place

before the storm?"

"He will not be afraid of the storm. He will stay, and I will watch with him as long as necessary. I will not leave him, but he would want you to be in where it is dry and warm."

Our precious Eliezer! Caring, as a son would, for Abram and me. I nodded my agreement to his suggestion that I go back to the security of the tent, and I smiled my appreciation for his staying with Abram.

Back in the tent I looked out at the sky. There was a continuous pulsating brilliance of summer lightning in the clouds and a sound of rushing wind, but no rain yet.

I left a lamp burning for Abram and was glad for its light. Nights were oppressively dark when there was no moon or starlight. The wind gradually subsided, but the darkness beyond the flare of the lamp seemed to have substance to it. It was eerie. I wanted Abram to come away from the field and forget this day which, so many hours ago, had begun with a camp-wide aura of excitement. I was exhausted, but sleep would not come. Remembering how relaxed Abram looked leaning against the tree, I thought now ironic it was—he, in the weather and in the place of frustration, could sleep; I, in my comfortable bed and in the protection of our tent, could not, not for several hours...not till the lamp went out.

Sleep finally came, and the sun was shining brightly when I awoke. Abram had come in and was sleeping soundly. I got up, dressed and left the tent quietly. I would find Eliezer, and he would tell me what—if anything— had happened.

He was checking supplies to be placed in packs for donkeys to carry to Hebron for a day of trading. He looked sleepy and a bit uneasy as I approached him with the questions he knew I would ask. "What happened? Did He come?"

Eliezer led me over to a place out of earshot of the men

working on the loading. We needed the quieter place, and he needed the time to think how to answer.

"I failed in my responsibility of watching. In spite of my best attempts to stay awake, I slept. No harm came to Abram, but when I awoke He was kneeling, with an uplifted, shining face. It seemed he saw beyond the heavens. He was blessing God, praising Him, vowing to be a good steward of the land and a good father to his household.

"I failed Abram and you. And I missed my great opportunity to see the glory of God!"

"Eliezer, you failed neither Abram nor me. I believe God wanted this covenant between Him and Abram to be private. I am sure that is why He waited until the rest of us were gone, until you were asleep, before He came. It seems to me that God is making a very special point, over and over, that He is dealing with one man for a unique purpose—and through him will bless everyone else, now and later. Don't fault yourself any more Eliezer. If you hadn't gone to sleep, Abram probably still would be waiting for his God to come!"

My words tumbled out in an effort to ease the sadness so evident in dear Eliezer's face. Perhaps they took away some of the feeling of guilt he had, but the thought of having almost seen the glory of God and missed the opportunity would continue to haunt him, I am certain.

He sighed, then managed a smile. It seemed he was relieved of some of his anxiety about falling asleep. "Is my master sleeping now?"

"Yes, I hope he will sleep until noon at least. I will go back to watch by the tent, making sure no one awakens him.

"Thank you, Eliezer, for being...so loyal to us." I had almost said, "for being like a son to us," but those words stopped somewhere in my throat and remained unspoken.

I sat down by our tent, beginning another kind of vigil. Neri came, and I walked out to meet him, telling him Abram could not be disturbed, that he needed a rest this morning.

Neri understood. I know he wanted to ask me questions about the outcome of the covenant ceremony, but he did not do so. I was glad because I had no answers then.

There were no more visitors. The morning hours slowly went by. If Abram hadn't awakened by noon I would have wakened him. I could not wait any longer to know what had happened.

I heard him moving around in the tent and looked in on him. He was like one in a trance, obviously so preoccupied with his thoughts that any questions from me would have been an inexcusable intrusion of privacy. He had met God alone in a dramatic event, and now, understandably, he struggled to assimilate his thoughts of it all.

Hardly realizing what he was doing, he reached for a cup of fruit juice I placed beside him. I refilled the glass after he drank it and gave him a slice of barley bread. He ate and drank in silence.

I went back to my room to give him time to think without pressure to explain anything, or to talk at all. I picked up the sash I was embroidering and began to put some stitches into it. I knew he would talk with me when he was ready and wouldn't even notice what I was working on; it could still be a surprise for him later.

I had waited for hours but suddenly he was there, standing in the doorway of my room, straight and tall and strong, looking as one whose eyes had seen such marvels that they could scarcely accommodate themselves to mundane things again.

"He came! He came!" Abram's voice choked with awe and victory.

"Before He came I had a vision. I had grown tired and had gone over to the shade of a tree to rest. It was getting dark and stormy. I thought I wouldn't have to chase those birds away any more; they would be heading for their nests. I intended to close my eyes for just a few moments, but I fell into a deep sleep and must have slept several hours. I heard

God explaining my vision. Was He there and I awake, seeing all this, or was He showing it all in a vision? That part is vague, but the things I saw were in sharp focus. What I heard Him say was clear.

"Sarai, He showed me that our descendants will be many indeed, and they will inherit this land. They will face terrors and afflictions and persecutions down through the years that I cannot speak of now, but He has promised deliverance from their tormentors and then great prosperity. He speaks in terms of generations—of hundreds of years—not in terms of months and years as we do. He spoke to me of our dear people for centuries to come. Their land, when they finally possess it in His good time, will be from the river of Egypt all the way across to the great river Euphrates! And I saw it!"

He stopped speaking, as if taking inventory of all he had said, and of what remained to be said. I was, by now, mirroring his dazed expression, unable to cope with the tremendous bad and good that was ahead for our people. Persecutions and possessions, God's foreknowledge of both, and His plan to work through it all! I felt a rush of excitement to hear what more Abram would tell me.

"At the time of making the actual covenant, there was a smoking pot with a blazing torch that passed between the carcasses of those animals. Symbolized by light, God entered into that covenant alone. He made it unilaterally, knowing I would never be able to keep my part of it perfectly. Our Covenant God has sealed His vows. Blessed be our God!"

16

...Sarai his wife took her Egyptian maidservant Hagar and gave her
to her husband to be his wife.   *Genesis 16:3*

*A*bram asked me to bring him a sheet of the papyrus we brought from Ur. Our supply was nearly gone even
though he used it only for his most important records, such
as the contract just made. He had labored for hours over the
words he would write. First he phrased and rephrased them
in his mind. Then he prayed to God Most High to guide him
in the actual writing. Finally he wrote the words on clay
tablets of the type used for everyday business matters. Again
he prayed, read it over, made a few changes, and was finally
satisfied. Now he was ready to copy it, painstakingly, on the
papyrus. The most difficult part had been keeping out his
own comments and reactions to so great an experience. His
finished record was accurate but extremely concise to
conserve precious space.

With a contented sigh, indicating he was released from
the tension of writing, he gave the record to me to put with
his other writings in his olivewood box. This cache of
writing was his most prized possession. When he moved, a
special guard was assigned to it. When we were in encampments, it rested in a secret hiding place.

The writing session completed, Abram relaxed into great
good humor which was contagious. Even though we remained at a loss to explain how things would be carried out,
we claimed the reenforced promises. The reason for the
delays, Abram thought, was so our faith could grow

stronger. I hoped with all my heart that our faith had now reached maturity!

Abram and I spent the whole day together. We walked through the camp, stopping to talk with the servants, many of whom were like family and very dear friends.

We walked out to the altar. Abram prayed to God, thanking Him for His love and protection and for His promises. On the way back from the altar I was so happy about everything that words just poured into my mind, and I said them aloud, "All praise to our God, whose love is our strength and life." I said the words over and over. As I repeated them, a melody line sprang up from my heart, and I sang for joy. Abram sang along with me. We kept singing, making up new phrases and adding them to the song. And as we sang, our joy opened a storehouse of long-forgotten and half-forgotten things for which to praise Him. We sang and danced and praised our God with the spontaneous delight of children.

We stopped, out of breath, filled with joy!

I am sure part of our happiness was geared to thinking that surely this time God's "yes" meant "now." That was certainly the case with me. I was not prepared for any more waiting. But it became evident that waiting was still what we must do. From the heights of the exhilaration I experienced that evening when we sang and danced, I went into a deep, draining depression. I moved from periods of impatience — wanting to do anything except wait — to periods of dejection when I didn't want even to move or to think. I felt more and more lonely, even when Abram was around.

Months after the covenant was made we still waited for our heir and for the actual possession of even an inch of ground. We rented fields from Ephron. We relied on the youthful support of Eliezer. I wondered how Abram could be so content. I even wondered if such contentment could be a virtue!

Maybe Abram should do something about acquiring the land. But what? Purchase it? Not even with all our wealth! Go to war? No, not without God's leading and we wouldn't have that. In response to my anxiety about the land Abram told me that part of his vision on that memorable day was that the sin of the Amorite nation had not yet reached its full measure. Until that time, God would hold back the forces that would later be unleashed against them.

Abram was satisfied that the land—all of it—was for us and for our descendants, in God's time. Descendants! What descendants? Abram was 85 and I, 75. Even if we lived to the age of our forefathers, we were past any possibility of having children. Abram might yet father a child but I was past the age of childbearing.

That idea churned in my mind until it occurred to me that God had never promised I would have a child! Each promise was to Abram alone. Perhaps I was not included in the plan. I could not stand the jolting pain that went though me as that thought persisted. I had stood by Abram in everything. I had given up home and loved ones. I had risked with him the misadventure in Egypt. Would I not share in the utmost blessing of having a child? I cared more about this than I cared about acquiring all the land! God's promises of an heir had kept my hopes alive longer than they normally would have survived. Most women would have, years before, stopped dreaming of a baby. My dreams aggravated the hurt. And now, were my dreams to die with the unsettling realization that their fulfillment was never ever meant to be? Was God's promise just for Abram? Had he thought of that, too, but out of love for me never mentioned it?

For the first time in my life, I wanted to die. Even in Pharaoh's palace, when I knew I might be trapped into an intolerable existence as one of his wives, the love of life surged through me with such force that I desperately prayed to escape, to live my life in freedom. Never did I even think of wanting to die.

Other women who had the stigma of childlessness solved it easily according to Sumerian laws and the accepted customs of the local sheikhs. A woman would have one of her servants become her husband's second wife. Any children born of that union became legally her own. It could be arranged so secretly that people did not know for certain that the baby was not really her own natural child. I had a handmaiden. I would speak with Abram about her, but first I would talk to Hagar.

Hagar had been coming every afternoon since I had been feeling so badly. She massaged my back and combed my hair, and we even had some short conversations. On that unforgettable day as she entered the tent she looked especially beautiful. She wore a pale yellow fringed dress and a light shawl over her head because of the cool breeze that was sweeping across the fields. The traditional dress of the local women did not become her as much as the exotic tunics she wore in Egypt, fastened on one shoulder, the other shoulder bare—rich embroidery on the hem and sash, and from the shoulder diagonally as the tunic draped under the other arm. But even in the more modest attire she was strikingly attractive, naturally sensuous. She was young and strong and confident—qualities I had known before but were lacking in all I had become.

Refreshed by the massage and the improved state of my hair I strove for composure to begin a conversation from which there could be no turning back to any previous relationship Hagar and I had known up to this point.

"Hagar, there is something I want to say to you, and it is most important. Please sit down on those pillows and be comfortable."

I could have stopped the conversation here, said I had changed my mind about talking to her, and dismiss her. A few more words and it would be too late. Then the words I had rehearsed tumbled out with no further thought!

"Since we first met many things have happened to change the course of our lives from what we thought would be. For you it has been the disappointment of not becoming the handmaiden of Pharaoh's wife and your less exciting life here in Canaan.

"It is too late to do anything about your disappointments. You will never have the high position you wanted at the Pharaoh's court. Since you were his slave, you could not return to any freedom in Egypt. As a slave there—demoted to carrying food and water to the road builders—your life would be harder than if you stay with us. It seems you have little choice."

I had to be certain Hagar understood she was well off with us and that any thought of a return to Egypt was an impractical fantasy. She had clung to her Egyptian ways as much as possible, treating servants from Canaan and Mesopotamia as though she were their superior because of her more sophisticated background. She did not look sophisticated at that moment. My words had cut deeply.

"Hagar, I have had disappointments in my life, too. Things are not all the way I wanted them. My biggest disappointment is that by now I had hoped to have fine sons and daughters, yet I have not given my husband even one heir."

I stopped speaking in spite of my plan to say it all quickly. I could still keep this to only a sharing of mutual sorrows. But Abram, my husband, deserved a son. Tears were welling up in my eyes, but I fought them back. I stood taller, took a deep breath, and plunged ahead to finish what I must say.

"I have not produced an heir, but it is within my power to arrange for him to have his son."

Hagar stiffened her back and raised her chin with a look that was a mixture of fear and defiance. She knew what I meant at once.

"The custom of the people is this land is that when a

woman is barren, she may give her handmaiden to her husband so there will be an heir. I have decided the time has come for this to be done in the house of Abram, and I have chosen you, Hagar, for this honor.

"I will speak to Abram about it tonight and will send him to you."

Tensions in the room were enormous. I believe we both wanted to cry, or scream, or run away. We merely faced each other with as little indication of inner feelings as possible.

"You may go now, Hagar."

She got up from the cushions gracefully, without speaking, not taking her eyes from my face. She looked at me in disbelief and then in open contempt. I handed her a box I had kept for a long time, never opened. Inside the box was a veil with patterns of gold leaf and a sprinkling of tiny white sapphires. She would recognize it as soon as she saw it.

I watched her walk back toward her tent, head erect, shoulders slightly swinging, her step light. Suddenly I heard a gale of laughter, and in it was mingled derision and anguish, or so I thought. I had done what I had thought might be impossible — I had humbled myself before Hagar.

I felt wretched and faced yet a worse ordeal in a few hours, when I would have to confront Abram with what I had done.

I prepared the evening meal mechanically and made no attempt to talk while we ate supper or after we finished. I wanted him to ask why I was so quiet, and he did.

"Sarai, why so serious tonight?"

"I am serious many times, and usually it is about the same problem."

"Dearest, I know what you mean, and I am at a loss to know how to console you. We have talked this over so often. I can only say again the summary of it all: I love you more than my own life; I love my unborn heir with greatest devotion. You are both in God's stated plan, and I leave you both in His keeping."

"Thank you, Abram, for saying it all again and saying it so well that I am almost of a mind not to tell you what I did today."

"Now you have my interest! What could you have done? It sounds exciting. We have no secrets from each other. Tell me!"

Abram was making an attempt to turn the conversation to a lighter vein, but it would not turn, for I would see this thing through now!

"First I will explain why I have come to the decision I have made. God said you would be father of this people that will be His own; He never said I would be the mother. His dealings have been with only you.

"Perhaps the reason we went to Egypt was to add to our household one who would be a suitable mother for your child. As you know, we did bring back with us my maidservant, Hagar. I am sure you have noticed her unusual beauty, and when you have talked with her, you must have been impressed that she is a young woman of great intelligence, wit, and resourcefulness.

"She is the one I choose to bear your son in my place."

Abram's deep voice filled the room, and surely the surrounding fields, "I want no other wife but you. Our God has different standards for us than our neighbors in this land have for themselves. I want no child by any one else while you are my wife—which will be, God willing, for all my years!"

He was making it hard for me. He said all the right things to make me want his arms around me, to make me know the warmth of his nearness. It would melt the icy chill that all but engulfed me when I thought of the end of this situation I was developing.

He had stated his love and his high principles and thought the matter had ended, as it had been ended many times before, at least temporarily. This time it would be different. I had one remaining argument, to be spoken softly.

"Abram, dearly beloved Abram, listen to me. I am giving Hagar to you because I love you; you are to take her to yourself because you love me and will free me from the torture of our childlessness. I beg you to take Hagar very soon—tonight—to have this over and done."

I had said it all without looking at Abram, for if I had seen the hurt I knew would be in his eyes I could not have done it.

Without speaking again, he went out into the night. I wondered if he had gone stumbling through the dark all the way to his altar, or if he had gone to Hagar.

I didn't know how it would finally work out, but I knew that three persons would never feel the same about each other as they had before. I could not decide if I had done right or wrong, but I had done the only thing I knew to break the endless years of longing for a child for Abram.

Now, where was Abram? How soon would I see him again? How would I face him? What would he say to me? I wanted—more than ever—to die. I looked at the chest that held the medicines I used when our people were ill.

I could take enough of some of it to.... No! I rejected that idea at once. I still wanted to die, but not badly enough to do that! I did take just enough of a medication so I would sleep for a while. I could not face this long night without that help.

_____ *17*

Abram was 86 years old when Hagar bore him Ishmael.

Genesis 16:16

*T*he next morning came—and the next, and the next, and the next. I prepared the meals. Abram had his business interests. We hardly spoke to each other. Trivial matters were not worth the energy it took to voice them. The important things were too painful to consider. I could not ask him if he had been with Hagar, and he did not tell me. Alternately, I hoped my plan had worked, and that it had failed.

Hagar did not come back to me for my massages, manicures, and hairwashings. Had our last communication been too painful for her to forgive? Had she come to think she was now above me in status? One particularly warm afternoon I sent for her.

"Hagar, have you been ill? I have missed your visits. My hair needs washing very badly."

"Then wash it! I have not felt well, nor do I feel well today. With—or without—your permission I will go back to my tent to rest."

That incident stands out in my mind, but it was only one of many, before and after that. I could have handled a few abrasive situations, but these were not occasional flare-ups of volatile personality. They were expressions of one who despised me and was motivated by vengeance. I felt too much a cause of her present indisposition to chide her or discipline her, but the atmosphere between us had to change. Perhaps a third person, a very wise third person, could mediate.

"Abram, Hagar is insolent and lazy. Have you given her reason to think she is above me? She treats me with disdain, and she neglects her duties to me. Are you not the master of this household, and will you not reprimand her?"

"What are you saying? Hagar is undisciplined? Then discipline her yourself. She knows how to do your bidding!"

I turned abruptly from Abram and hurried to Hagar's tent. His uncaring words disturbed my mind, and his angry tone of voice rang in my ears.

I can't remember all I said to her, but it was a tirade! Hagar bore the brunt of my anger at her for the way she had always assumed attitudes unbecoming a servant, of my anger at Abram for his recent lack of companionship with me, and of anger at myself for the way I had allowed my personality to be eroded by frustration and by useless anger at God for withholding His promises.

Never before had I ranted at such length, berating her for real and imagined slights, for her blunders and her insubordination. My anger fed on itself and although I wanted to feel totally in charge of the moment, I knew I was not even in control of myself.

When I had talked myself out, Hagar, who had listened without change of expression, stood up and very deliberately walked to a reed basket by her bed. She took from it that veil and draped in tantalizingly over her face. She tossed her head back, and I heard again her wild laughter. I rushed to her in blind rage and slapped her face, then ran from her tent. I never wanted to see her again. I would have her sent back to Egypt—to Haran—anywhere.

The following morning Hagar was missing from the camp. No one had seen her leave; no one knew where she might have gone. Frantically, Abram organized search teams to scout the area for her. I was thoroughly frightened and hoped Abram did not know I had been so harsh with her. I was thankful he did not know I had determined to have her out of our camp.

I worried about what the servants knew of all the trouble involving Hagar and made it a point that day to ask about it. "Nika, there is no word yet from Hagar. Why do you think she ran away? Have you talked with anyone who might have an idea?"

"I have talked with several, mistress, but their ideas are so unbelievable that I would not repeat them to you."

"Thank you, Nika. I detest gossip." I turned quickly from her, hoping the flush I felt in my cheeks had not been apparent to her, verifying the gossip.

Hagar came back by herself two days later. She walked to my tent and straight into my room. She looked so very weak and exhausted that I got up and offered her a mat to sit on and poured a cup of water for her. I waited for her to speak.

"I managed to get back with no one seeing me. I will not try to explain all that happened after I ran away, but He told me to come back to you. When He says to do something, you just know you have to do it."

"Who told you to come back to me? Where did you go? Abram sent many men to search for you, but they came back without finding any trace of you. We were all worried."

"I meant that you should worry and search — and never find me. But I was not very clever. Neither were your scouts. I went to the most probable place — the edge of the Wilderness of Shur. When I came to that same well where we stopped on our way here from Egypt, He was there. He called me by name. He told me what I already knew — that I must not try to cross that desert alone. He told me to come back to you and to be more submissive to you. I thought that unfair unless He also told you to treat me differently, but I didn't say so. He is not one you contradict!"

"Hagar, who was he? Who spoke to you?"

"He spoke as a man, and yet He was not just a man. He

knew all things about me, and He knows the future. He said the son I would bear would be wild and obstinate. I am to name him Ishmael, because the Lord has heard my affliction!"

"Who told you all this?" I whispered the question this time, not daring to trust my full voice because I was trembling with apprehension.

"You should know. I have listened to you speak of your God. You said He has blessing for all people. I say it was He who spoke to me at the well and I call Him 'God who sees me.'"

My mind was whirling. Had God spoken to her? He had not ever spoken to me! I wanted to challenge her statements. I did not believe God spoke to her; I didn't want to believe it. I decided to change the subject.

"I am relieved that you are back, Hagar. I will tell Abram. God has given us another chance to mend the hurts between us. Go now and rest. You no longer need to be my personal maid. Prepare things for your child. There will be a maidservant available to you from now on. Do you have a preference from among the women?"

"No—anyone who will serve me with the proper care and skill. The God who sees me turned me back from what would have been certain death in that wilderness of sand. This is as it should be. My child, Abram's son and heir, should have his chance at life. Have my maidservant come to me as soon as possible."

She left immediately, as one who had just given orders to a slave. The last time we met, I had slapped her face; this time I felt as though she had slapped mine, hard!

The next months passed slowly. I spent a lot of time thinking of people and things far removed from the tense atmosphere of the camp at Mamre. I thought of old Abutab and Inmashagger, Terah's faithful servants who had stayed at Haran with Nahor. Were they still alive? We had not heard from Nahor and Milcah for so long. Maybe they were not even alive. Had they continued to prosper? What if they could see wealthy Abram and me now — the part of their family who left old securities to follow the one God and found a great nation! We had not done much in that regard, but now, after a fashion, Abram's dynasty might soon begin.

What about Lot? I never did know the name of his wife. She should have been like a daughter-in-law to me. Had they ever wanted to come to see us? What had kept them away? Did he still follow the one God or had the taint of Sodom's immorality overcome him and his sons and daughters? Sons and daughters . . . Everyone should have at least one son. Abram would have his soon.

I tried to think of people and places who had no connection with "here and now," but no matter — every evasion turned into a direct route back to what I tried not to think about.

I went into Hebron with some maidservants and Zaccur and his men, bought a low acacia-wood table and two straight chairs on short legs to match. I would have things if not family. Abram did not like the furniture, and we did not keep it long. It was too large for our tent anyway.

Abram did not speak of going to his altar. If he went, he must not have seen his God or had his usual time of joyful praise there, for he never had that hint of music in his voice now, nor the look of peace and glory on his face.

I did not go to visit Hagar. I never spoke of her to anyone. I knew she was getting along well for God was watching over her!

Those months were endless for all of us.

Just after Abram's 86th birthday Hagar bore Abram's son and called him by the name the angel of the Lord had given — Ishmael.

. . . you are no longer to call her Sarai; her name will be Sarah. I will bless her and will surely give you a son by her. I will bless her so that she will be the mother of nations; kings of peoples will come from her.
Genesis 17:15-16

*I*shmael was a beautiful child—tan skin, dancing dark eyes, a finely formed mouth that was made to smile and laugh. He was a happy boy with boundless energy—and a mind that was quick to channel that energy into mischief! He was the pet of the whole camp but had such engaging good humor that it was impossible not to be amused by him even when he was teasing people with his jokes.

Abram saw him every day he was not away from camp on business, and there was a good rapport between the two. Even before Ishmael learned to talk he seemed to communicate with his father with his eyes, and Abram was his devoted servant. He watched his son grow and learn to walk. He was thrilled to hear his first words. I seldom saw the boy.

When Ishmael was ten, Abram gave him a donkey to ride and allotted him his own servant companion. Ishmael was born to the saddle and spent hours at a time riding with his companion across the fields—sometimes going into Hebron. But that was without permission.

Two years later Ishmael persuaded Abram to replace the donkey with a camel. Abram gave him a fine young one with elaborate red and white leather harness and saddle. There was also a camel for Ishmael's companion. Ishmael had several companions. He rode so hard, played so hard, and contrived so many jokes on them that each one in succession asked to be relieved of the honor of serving him to become shepherds or to work in the fields.

One of the strongest memories I have of Ishmael is the way he and his current companion would ride through the camp and out onto the road or across the fields on those camels.

Often Abram rode with them, and they would adjust their speed to the pace he set. As they rode together, Abram taught Ishmael about the land—how to survive on it and where to find the best game for hunting.

This boy, at first an embarrassment to him, quickly became one of his chief delights. Abram took pride in his alert mind, his strength, and his independence.

"I am teaching him mathematics, and he is a ready learner."

"That's good."

"He handles donkeys and camels better than any other boy of his age."

"That's nice."

"He wants me to allow him and his companion to go on an overnight trip. Then, when they can accomplish that, he wants to ride to Gerar!

"Why not let him? His companion will assist him, if he needs any help."

Abram often talked to me of Ishmael. I tried to be polite but never encouraged the conversations. They always made me feel uncomfortable. I resented the boy but wanted to love him for Abram's sake.

Hagar and I avoided each other as much as possible. She worked with the women who wove tent material. I imagined how she would chatter on and on to the women about her son, Abram's only heir. She made it a point to walk grandly with him through the camp frequently. He grew more handsome with each year, but I saw little resemblance to Abram.

Abram, skillful in managing herds and in merchandising,

was one of the most successful businessmen in the Hebron area. These interests, and the hours he spent with Ishmael, left us little time together, but our feelings which had been trampled on more than a dozen years ago had mended. We had long since stopped speaking of it except in indirect reference when he talked about Ishmael. Our love was stronger than the hurts we caused each other, and our relationship regained its beauty and strength.

We spoke of God Most High in our conversations; we worshiped only Him. But we seldom mentioned His promises any more.

I looked at Abram as he stood in the doorway, turning to wave a good-bye. He was making a routine visit to the altar. "Abram, my husband, you stand as tall and walk as straight as you did when you checked out the caravans in Ur."

"Look closer, Sarai. Make sure you are seeing with your eyes and not with your imagination." Abram laughed, but I knew he was pleased with the compliment.

"I will be there all day and maybe most of tomorrow. I plan to stay overnight at least. The longing to see my Friend is overwhelming, and in times long past that was an indication He will appear to me with a special word. It has been so very long since He has spoken."

I smiled somewhat cynically inside, wondering if He would tell Abram again that he would have the honor of being the father of many, now that he had one son. But I only said, "I will miss you, Abram. May you receive the blessing you seek from El Elyon."

He did stay overnight as he had said, and it was late the next afternoon when he came back. I was sitting in front of our tent, watching for him. When he saw me he began to run, with head thrown back and arms waving in excitement.

Before he caught his breath he began to talk, "Our God was truly calling me to meet with Him. He was there! He was there! He told me wonderful things—more detailed than ever before. I have so much to tell you I don't know how to begin. He spoke of you and called you by name — by two names!"

"Two names?"

"Yes. Oh, there was so much He said that I am reeling from the excitement of it."

"And you have had no sleep. You are hungry. I want to hear all you have to say, but first eat something and rest a while. There will be time for talking later."

Abram sat down on some cushions, only then realizing how tired he really was. I left him to prepare some food, and when I came back he was barely awake.

"Sarai, the blessings He spoke of are unimaginably price-less — for us both!"

"Don't try to tell me now. Wait until you have eaten and are rested." I was in no hurry to hear; I had heard promises before. Abram's enthusiasm had not found its counterpart in me this time.

I went outside to look at the stars. "El Elyon, are they tokens of our promised descendents looking down at me with twinkling eyes? 'Look up at the heavens and count the stars. . . . So shall your offspring be.' You said that to Abram. I am sorry, my God, I cannot count them because my eyes are blurred with these tears."

Abram would have been finished with his supper by then, and I thought of going back inside to hear his newest message from God, but decided against it. I would wait until morning. I looked away from the stars and my eyes fell on a section of camp where Hagar and Ishmael lived.

Then Abram called me, softly, haltingly, "Do not plan to bake bread . . . or weave . . . or anything else tomorrow. I will tell you your new name . . . and my new name . . . ."

I ran back in to see why he had not finished the sentence. He was asleep.

Before breakfast he was eagerly telling me of all our God had said. It became so exciting that we never did eat break-fast — and did not even notice!

"We have a wondrous new name by which to call Him — El Shaddai, God Almighty. We have known of His ultimate power, His perfect knowledge, His being everywhere, and His having created all things. Now, He has included all this and more in this new name which He revealed to me. When I say 'El Shaddai,' I feel in my mind and soul the vibrant, absolute authority of the divine One who said His name that speaks of perfect command.

"When He gave His name as El Shaddai, He also gave me understanding that He is a God who not only created the world and fixed its natural laws, but a God who can overrule His own natural laws, making things behave differently. His highest creatures, man and woman, are designed for reproduction according to set natural laws, but even here He is not bound to what we call natural means. He can change this fundamental process when He pleases!

"I want to say this in such high phrases, but none are high enough! So I will bring it down to a homely comparison. It is as though you, Sarai, are going to make one of your fine cakes. You have developed a pattern by which you make them all. But you want one in particular to be the best ever made because it is for a unique celebration. Would you not alter your recipe to allow it to be made with finer flour, sweeter honey, or whatever you chose, knowing it would be so great no one would know how you had done it?

"Sarai... God is going to overrule a basic, natural process in your life. The result will be a son so fine that he will be the planned link in His promises for mankind. This son will be born in such a dramatic way that for all time to come people will marvel, knowing only El Shaddai could have intervened to allow it to happen."

The indifference I had felt about hearing his report dissolved! I leaned forward and took his hand to steady myself, almost afraid of what he would say next but scarcely able to wait for him to say it. But then, after getting my very undivided attention when he spoke of a miraculous birth of a baby, he went on a tangent of equal amazement!

"El Shaddai—I actually trembled in awe in His presence, conscious as never before of His unfathomed power and majesty and provision—gave a command. 'Walk before me and be blameless.'"

"Blameless! Abram, how? US? Blameless?"

"Those are His words."

"Is this a condition to be met to obtain His promises? Then His promises, I know for certain, are not for me. I will never grow in faith and obedience enough to be blameless! You might, but not I." Hot tears were stinging the corners of my eyes, and I felt that if this was one more time of building up to a wonderful hope only to fall into another despair, I could not survive it.

"Sarai, His promise is already made and confirmed. He has bound Himself to it! Remember how He sealed the covenant Himself, walking alone through the emblems of the binding contract? It is a right response to that magnificent love that we should want to be at our best as we represent Him, being His people."

"But blamelessly?"

Abram smiled a little sadly and answered, "He knows us too well to think we will ever perfectly represent Him if we live in Canaan to be as old as my forefather, Methuselah! But by divine command we must take perfection as our goal—take it seriously enough that we make trying for anything less unthinkable."

He stopped speaking. A quizzical look on his face told me he was not satisfied with how he had explained all this. He held up his hand for me to be quiet while he thought about it, then closed his eyes to concentrate. After some moments when I thought he must have gone to sleep, he slowly opened shining eyes, and a smile softened the lines in his face.

"I will have to use everyday examples again, Sarai, for every time I try to sound lofty I say things only half as well.

"Think of a white almond blossom, beautiful in the late winter or early spring—perfect. But later, when it is time for fruit to have developed, if it is still only a blossom, then it is no longer perfect, for it should have been an almond by then. So, when we begin to obey our God, we may be perfect for beginners, but we must go on to become what he intends for us to be."

"Are you saying we are in the process of growing up—maturing—or should be?"

"Exactly. And I do not come to these conclusions because of any unusual intellect of my own. As I hear Him speak, He gives me understanding of what He is saying. He will not expect the impossible of us; neither will He be satisfied with anything less than all we can become.

"It comes to my mind that He must be much more disappointed in the slow progress we make in our life of faith and obedience than we could ever be because His promises to us seem delayed."

That was a new thought for me. I had found it easy to think of how long God was keeping us waiting, but had been far less concerned about His disappointment at the frequent unevenness of my temper and my restlessness.

"Abram, no wonder you stay so long when God meets you at the altar. There is so much to understand about His words. I am eager to hear all you have to say, but pace your conservation slowly because I am trying to absorb in minutes what came to you in many hours! Abram, no matter how you phrase it or illustrate it, it is a staggering thought that El Shaddai calls us to walk perfectly before him!" Then I couldn't keep from smiling at something that came into my mind. "At one time I would have thought perfection meant having the poise and charm of a goddess. Since I can now recognize that as a childish thought, I can see I have been learning some things—even if my learning has been slow and my application of the learning even slower.

"I can remember when I thought my life was going to

regress into boredom with no challenges. But since leaving Ur I have found more challenges than I have been able to meet!"

"That's why it's good to know that this wonderfully challenging God is also our Friend. Keep remembering His solitary walk the day of the covenant ritual, pledging Himself to utter faithfulness, already knowing what our meager response would be." Abram was weeping; he brushed at his face with a rough, sun browned hand.

"My dearest, we could keep talking about this, but we will have to come back to it in other days. I must go on to tell you the exciting things that are clustered in my mind, impatient to be expressed.

"He gave me a new name—Abraham—meaning 'father of many.'" Abram looked absolutely pleased. I was not.

"Your old name, Abram, meant 'exalted father' and it was a cause of derision for years and years when you had no son. Now, 'father of many'—Abraham! People will think you have gone mad. You finally have one son and would call yourself by so high a name!"

"I know the joking that has gone on about my name, and I am certain it will increase with my greater name. But it is my pledge of faith in God's word that I let myself be thought a fool by accepting the name He offers."

Abram had said God had new names for both of us. I did not care to find out what mine was. I could not take the ridicule as easily as Abram.

"Sarai, you are not listening to me! How can you not pay attention?"

"My mind speaks back to me as it is forced to accept new things. Right now it does not want to call you a new name—or accept a new one for me."

"I haven't even told you your name yet! Your mind will be most happy with it. Let me finish with the part about me. Then I will get to the part about you."

Abram—Abraham—went on to tell me that El Shaddai again vowed he would be exceedingly fruitful. Some of his descendants would be kings. The covenant for possession of the land by Abraham's offspring was an everlasting one. Then he told that God commanded a physical sign of separation to Himself, a symbolic pledge of purity and obedience. The symbol was the rite of circumcision for every male, a sign carved into their flesh, reminding them of their holy relationship with God.

And then—he turned to the messages God had for me. The first was my new name. I had been sure it would imply a great demotion from Sarai, "like a princess," because of my behaviour regarding Hagar and because of the general shallowness of my faith. I could no longer seem "like a princess" to El Shaddai—or even to myself. I loved that name though, even when I didn't live up to it. I wanted to keep it.

In telling me of the name, Abraham used the very words of El Shaddai, as they had been impressed on his mind in the glowing moment they were first spoken. "As for Sarai your wife, you are no longer to call her Sarai; her name will be Sarah. I will bless her and will surely give you a son by her. I will bless her so that she will be the mother of nations; kings of peoples will come from her."

I covered my mouth with both hands to keep from saying anything to detract from that moment. I closed my eyes and felt sweet, warm tears stream across the wrinkles in my cheeks. It was unbelievable, yet I did not doubt it. "Abraham" and "Sarah" embraced and neither of us spoke for a very long while.

"Abram—Abraham—will you say all that again, and again . . . please."

He repeated it, word for word, until I could say it with him. I truly believed it, but did Abraham believe it too? What had his reaction been to my bearing a child?

"Tell me, what did you think when He told you about me?"

Smile lines crinkled around his eyes, and quite contentedly he seemed to be trying to picture that scene. "When He told me your new name, I was so ecstatic that I bowed before Him in glad adoration and praise. Then, as he continued to speak and said you would become a mother — and it was not just your age I was thinking about, Sarah; it was both of us, at our ages, having a child—Oh, Sarah! I was so shocked I literally toppled over, and in the storm of emotions I was experiencing—joy, doubt, faith—and fear that I might not have heard correctly—I fell on my face and laughed!"

"Laughed? Abraham! You didn't!"

"Yes, I did. And it was not displeasing to El Shaddai, for He immediately told me we should name our son Isaac, meaning, of course, 'laughter.'"

"A son! A son named laughter! Yes, that is an appropriate name, for while we are laughing with delight there will be others who laugh in derision, considering us freaks of nature."

"Only those who do not understand our God will laugh, Sarah, and we can hope that through the very miracle of what they deride, they will come to see, unmistakably, the hand of God Almighty, El Shaddai!"

"Our son, Isaac! My own baby! I feel years roll away from me as I think of him. I actually feel younger, and there is a strength deep inside me I have not been aware of before. Do I even look younger, Abraham?"

"My princess, you are always young and beautiful to me! But Sarah, let me say one more great thing from our God. Hear His words: 'My covenant I will establish with Isaac, whom Sarah will bear to you by this time next year.'"

"Next year? Next year? He has set the time? It is definite? Next year! Abraham, I never knew such joy was possible!"

"It is becoming clear how we are to be the source of blessings for all nations, Sarah. It will not be fulfilled in our generation, but we will have begun a line through which the covenant of promise will be handed down until all nations are blessed by our descendants—even by the kings among them!"

"And it will be through a miraculous birth to parents beyond natural ability to conceive and bear children that it shall come. Our waiting for a son was this long so God can demonstrate that it is by His divine intervention that our son exists. By this son, Isaac, generations to come will know God did choose us, worked through us, and will work through Isaac and his descendants. Blessed be the name of our God!"

"Yes, blessed be His name, El Shaddai the Almighty. And blessed are Abraham, Sarah, and their son, Isaac."

We could talk of little else for days afterwards, and even when we were not talking of it, I thought about it.

"I will be going to the altar in the morning, Sarah, to offer the very finest lamb of our flock in thanksgiving to our God for our son, Isaac, who will be dedicated to Him."

"May I go with you to share in this sacrifice of praise?"

"Yes, we will go together, early tomorrow morning."

19

Is anything too hard for the Lord?   *Genesis 18:14*

"How is Milzah? Did you help her?" Abraham, sitting in the shade of our tent, called to me as I came back from Milzah's tent one witheringly hot morning. I had been called to go to this maidservant who was in severe pain from an old injury to her back. I had used a poultice that eased her pain many times before and planned to go back to see her again later in the day if she needed further help.

"I hope I helped her, Abraham. I will know later on. The walk over there and back has tired me out. I am going inside to rest now."

"Pull the sleeping mat out where it will be in the path of a breeze if one comes by, Sarah. It is very hot in that tent!"

It was a good suggestion, and I hoped there would be many breezes! It felt good to rest, even without them. I was glad Abraham was staying in that shady spot outside for it was much too warm for him even to consider venturing out on his regular tour of the pasturelands.

Suddenly he scrambled to his feet and called to me, in disbelief, "There are three men walking toward our tent from the roadway. I do not recognize them, and yet it seems . . . it seems I should know them."

"Walking? In this heat? Who would be doing that? They are not riding camels or donkeys?"

"No, walking—right toward our tent, rapidly."

I hoped he was mistaken about what he saw. If there were men coming, they would need hospitality—food and something to drink. But I was tired. I let my eyes close and felt drowsy immediately.

My rest was short-lived, for in what seemed like no time at all I heard his voice coming through my sleepy haze. "If I have found favor in your eyes, my Lord, do not pass your servant by. Let a little water be brought, and then you may all wash your feet and rest under this tree. Let me get you something to eat, so you can be refreshed and then go on your way — now that you have come to your servant."

The intense eagerness in Abraham's voice surprised me as much as his offer of such gracious hospitality on so warm a day! He was overjoyed to see these people. Yet only a few minutes before he had not recognized who they were. He pled with them to stay and accept the very best we had to offer. I knew that his "something to eat" meant one of my finest cakes. I held my breath to hear what they would answer — to learn if they would stay or be gone. I was hoping they had business too urgent to allow them to wait for any cake baking. I peeked through the doorway just as they replied, "Do as you say."

"They" said it — but as with a single voice! With a burst of excitement I remembered Abraham had addressed these three as "my Lord" — as though he also saw the three but considered them one. What was this mystery?

I pulled back from the door just as Abraham rushed in excitedly. "Quick, get three seahs of fine flour and knead it and bake cakes on the hearth — your finest cake of the finest flour, Sarah!"

Before I could answer, he ran from the tent in the direction of the nearest herd. He brought back a young, tender calf and gave it to a manservant to have it dressed at once and prepared on the spit in the grandest manner for a feast.

At least a dozen of us scurried around to make things as festive as Abraham intended they should be. While we worked, the guests rested in the shade of some almond trees nearby.

At last the meal was ready: meat, cakes, the best wine, the choicest fruit and vegetables available—all served with as much style as possible. Abraham looked pleased with it and called his friends to come and dine.

Leaving Josah to wait further on them, I went from the room where they were dining, back through Abraham's room, and into mine in the back of the tent. From there I heard only muffled conversation during the meal which would last for hours. The sun would go down soon, but I had sent several young boys with woven reed fans to help circulate the air and make the dining area more comfortable. I was almost too exhausted to rest when I first allowed myself the ease of the sleeping mat, but, relieved that the day was ending, I began to relax and even slept lightly at times. When I realized the voices were getting louder and it seemed the guests were preparing to leave, I got up, went to the door of my room, and listened intently. Then I walked through Abraham's room to the opening into where they sat, still listening.

One of the guests sensed I was eavesdropping and said, "Where is your wife Sarah?"

"If you look quickly you will see her watching at the door into this room," Abraham answered. His voice had the sound of a smile in it, as though he was pleased to know me so well he could know where I would be at any given moment!

The visitor continued, "I will return to you about this time next year, and Sarah your wife will have a son."

I laughed. I could not help it. I kept the laughter inside, but it was there! Hearing about my having a baby in the gentle words Abraham used was one thing; but hearing it from this stranger who did not even know me made it sound ridiculous! And how could he have guessed... unless ... could it be that I had prepared the cakes for... I could not bring myself to speak the holy name!

Then he asked, "Why did Sarah laugh and say, 'Will I really have a child, now that I am old?'"

How had he heard my silent laughter and my unspoken words! He was . . . I had seen . . . I was looking at an appearance of . . . I could not yet say His name, even to myself! Surely my heart was no longer beating—I felt like a hollow woman, weak and frightened at the thought of who was standing there, aware of my impertinent laughter. Since He knew I was there, I stepped into the doorway. He looked at me and said, "Is anything too hard for the Lord?"

In reverence, but with a boldness that surprised both Abraham and myself, I went out into the room. Very much afraid I had hurt His feelings and not wanting Him to think I was beyond believing I would bear a son—and thus to deny me that privilege—I whispered, "I did not laugh."

He continued to look at me. "Yes, you did laugh." He corrected me, but He spoke in great love. I knew He understood both my faltering words and my groping faith. He smiled His love and understanding right into my soul. I saw Him only that once, but it was enough. For the rest of my life I would not doubt Him or what He would do through Abraham and me. He had spoken to me; I had spoken to Him! I had been in direct contact with Reality for the first time in my life, and I never would be the same again. I felt the silly, self-important Sarai had finally given way to Sarah, who had given way to God the Almighty!

I bowed before Him—them. How could three persons be so like one? I intended to stay bowed until my emotions were under control, but as the men started to leave, I raised my eyes to see them one more time. They were walking toward the road, Abraham with them.

In a few moments Abraham was back, saying as he gathered up a few possessions and thrust them into a pack, "They will go toward Sodom. I will walk with them. I will be gone for a day or two—maybe more. Eliezer will go with me. We will start in these cool evening hours."

He had spoken in short, choppy sentences that matched his haste and his apprehension over what would happen when a holy almighty God confronted the depravity at Sodom.

Sodom—how had Lot ever chosen to live in that city? How could people have devised so wrong a set of values as those approved there? What kind of god could accept such behaviour?

Even though the ugliness of Sodom had been pushed into my mind by Abraham's going toward that place, it could not bother me for long. I had Isaac to think about—plans to dream of and preparations to make for his coming.

Then I thought of Milzah and wondered if the poultice had eased her. I had meant to go back to her, but in all the excitement it had slipped my mind. If she had needed me, surely her family would have come to say so. Would they have been reluctant to intrude on our guests. I picked up some lotions and herbs, put them into my medicine basket, and went to her.

She was resting better, but I applied the lotion to her back anyway. Then I walked back to my tent. It was dark except for the subtle, silver shine from the moon. The gentle beauty of the moonlight was nearly wasted on me for, aching with tiredness, I could not pay it proper attention.

Four days after leaving camp with his Lord, Abraham returned with Eliezer. Both looked solemn and saddened. In bits and pieces he told me that the Lord had shared with him the plan to destroy Sodom because of its wickedness. He had interceded with God on behalf of the city until he had God's promise that if there were even ten righteous people there, the town would be spared because of them.

"Wouldn't Lot and his family have made ten, counting the sons-in-law and his daughter-in-law that we have heard of?"

"Yes. That is why, when God promised to hold back his wrath for ten, I thought all would be safe. I believe Lot is faithful to God, but apparently he does not have enough influence over his own family, let alone the other people of the city, for them to be worshipers of our God."

Abraham struggled with the words that would confirm what was evident from his conversation thus far. "Since ten could not be found, the city was destroyed, totally. It was an awesome, frightening spectacle even from where I watched on a hill well-removed from Sodom. Fire and brimstone plummeted down on that city in a sudden deluge of such magnitude that no one could have escaped."

"And Lot and his family—what must have happened to them?"

"I have not heard from him, of course, but I believe God would have made provision for even one in that town who worshiped Him to be saved from the destruction. I believe with all my heart and mind that He would not have destroyed any person who, even weakly, followed Him and called Him the only true God. There is massive devastation around other cities in the plain. Sodom was not the only one involved. It will be a long, long time until we know for certain the extent of the catastrophe. No one can breathe the air around that area and survive now. Meanwhile, we trust Lot to his God."

Our good news had been tempered quickly by this sad news of darkest chaos. It was difficult to be sad and glad at the same time.

20

> By faith Abraham, even though he was past age — and Sarah herself was barren — was enabled to become a father because he considered him faithful who had made the promise.   *Hebrews 11:11*

*W*e received no word from Lot. There was a rumor he and most of his family had escaped from Sodom, but he had not communicated with us. Did he not understand we still worried about him, still cared for him?

In an attempt to break the tension, Abraham proposed that we move to another location, at least for a while. "Sarah, the pasturelands here at Mamre are wearing thin. We have been here for a long time, and I think we need a change of scene. Let's go to some other part of our land again. I can arrange to have Neri separate some herdsmen and their flocks. We will travel with them in caravan, as we used to do. We could go to the Negev, near Kadesh, Shur, and Gerar. Would you like that?"

"Yes, it would be like reliving a part of our life — an exciting part. How soon can we leave?"

"We will plan to leave within ten days."

It would be more like our previous life than we bargained for! When we were established in the grasslands around Gerar we began to hear rumors about Abimelech, the local tribal king. He had become impressed with the customs of Egypt, copying many of them — especially Pharaoh's custom of screening caravans to select women for his harem. I knew Abraham had heard the same rumors, but we did not speak of them to each other. It was too painful a subject, even after all the years that had passed. We were delighted to be back in the area and spent happy hours revisiting places we had seen before—the marketplace, the banks of the languid Besor River, and the outlying grasslands where we could watch the white oryx, the long-horned ibex, and the dainty-faced gazelles. Each day was beautiful.

One refreshingly cool evening Abraham and I were finishing supper, talking about the things we had seen that afternoon as we rode our donkeys out through the fields we had rented. He became quiet and stared at me as though he were seeing me for the first time. "Sarah, I know God is causing you to become able to bear a child. If I did not know this I would wonder at the radiance in your eyes and the lovely flush in your cheeks. The lines that had come in your face are disappearing and there is a youthful fullness to your face again."

Surely the flush in my cheeks was becoming even more evident as I heard Abraham's words. "This must be the result of so much happiness. I feel saturated with it!"

He went on as though I had not interrupted him. "In many ways you are more beautiful now than when you were a bride in Ur! Not only I notice this, but I have seen heads turn as we go through the market place, and I know they are not looking at me."

"Abraham, I will never be too old to enjoy compliments. Thank you for them. I must add something to what you have said. In addition to the way my appearance has changed, I feel so much better, too. I have not felt this young and vigorous for a long, long time. A walk across the fields, occasional caring for the sick, baking a cake—all these things had been tiring me. Now I have a new energy. Walking is a delight, and I believe I could even dance again. I am in love with you. I am in love with unborn Isaac. I am in love with life. I shall never be old again!"

My rejuvenation was real; it was God-given. It was

apparent enough not only to us, but to a few of Abimelech's men. They thought I was a woman who might appeal to their king. Without warning they rode into our camp the next day and said, "On orders from Abimelech, King of Gerar, you are to come with us."

Abraham, startled beyond measure, cried, "Don't take my sister!"

"Your sister?"

"Yes." Abraham almost whispered the word.

"Not your wife?"

"My . . . sister."

It had happened so fast; Abraham hadn't intended to say that! I wept for him and screamed in panic for myself!

"Quiet, woman," the guard shouted, then added as though trying to comfort me, "You will lack nothing at Abimelech's court."

Abimelech's palace was elegant, but could not compare with the splendor I remembered in Egypt. The procedure was the same, however, and I was not surprised to find myself hurried through the halls to the harem. Frightened, hardly able to realize where I actually was, I did not answer the questions being put to me. I ate no food. I drank only one tumbler of water from a pitcher a servant placed by my bed. There was a silver incense burner in the room, and the odor from the incense was sickeningly sweet.

When I had time to collect my thoughts, the predominate one was that El Shaddai said my son would be born. I found that a source of calmness. He had delivered me from mighty Pharaoh; He would deliver me from lesser Abimelech. And surely—oh, yes—He would forgive Abraham for lapsing into momentary fear. I knew that by now his fear would be gone, as mine was. I felt absolutely certain that my husband and I were of one mind in this—not filled with fear but with trust in God—as we again found ourselves in a situation beyond our own ability to resolve.

The words of my God, which I heard from His own lips,

sang in my mind, "Is anything too hard for the Lord?"

Nothing! Nothing is too hard for my God!

That same night He appeared to Abimelech in a dream, explaining about Abraham's relationship to me and threatening a curse over his house until the husband and wife were restored to each other.

I slept soundly that night. When I awakened, the peace God had given me still filled my heart. I had seen Him with my own eyes, heard His voice with my own ears. The faith I had now was stronger than when I heard of Him only through Abraham. It was as though I had evidence of things that as yet were not seen or understood—but certain nevertheless.

When a maidservant told me to prepare to enter Abimelech's great hall, and that Abraham was already there, I was not surprised. I dressed rapidly, prayed my thanks to God, and went with the servant.

It was quite a scene in that great palace! Abraham, with Eliezer beside him, stood before the king, listening to the enraged monarch upbraid him for his deception. The king's high officials, many of his servants, and I had been summoned to hear it.

Abraham found his courage, as I knew he would. He answered the wrath of the king with honesty and poise. He had looked humiliated when Abimelech first began his recital of grievances. Then he was obviously relieved when he heard of the imminent release and its generous terms.

Abimelech, up until that time, had no fear of our God. But now he was reminded of what had happened in Egypt years before, when Pharaoh learned of the power of the God of Abraham.

Like Pharaoh, he now wanted us to leave his palace. But he did not insist we leave his land. Instead, he offered us any place we wanted for our encampment. He had not given us a showy gift at the time of my abduction, but he gave a large gift of silver when he restored me to my husband as evidence that he was making amends for his rashness. And unlike

Pharaoh, he had Abraham pray for him.

A very humbled intercessor knelt to pray. He began hesitatingly, as one speaks to a Friend from an embarrassing situation. But as he prayed, he began to speak forcefully on Abimelech's behalf, praying for the king, his family, and his entire household. Then he lifted his hands in praise and shouted to El Shaddai, "Blessed, blessed, blessed is our God!"

21

Sarah...bore a son to Abraham in his old age, at the very time God
had promised him.   *Genesis 21:2*

*G*iven the opportunity to use the best grazing
area around Gerar, Abraham decided we should stay
indefinitely. He sent word back to Neri and Zaccur to
close out affairs at Mamre, break camp, and join us as
soon as possible. Hagar and Ishmael would be coming
also.

Settling into a new permanent camp took a lot of
Abraham's time, but he saw to it that his and Ishmael's
companionship did not deteriorate because of the imminent
coming of another son. He toured all the surrounding land
with the boy and continued to enjoy his sprightly wit, his
quickness to learn, and his carefree adjustment to his new
home. Perhaps Ishmael did not realize how altered his place
with Abraham would become, and it was just as well, for he
added pleasure to my husband's life.

Abraham also had time for me. I no longer went into
Gerar to shop, but when he went, he always brought back
some surprise for me—a special herb for tea, some wonderfully textured linen, an ornate fan, earrings with large amber
stones that seemed to flash from their own inner source of
light. He was devoted to me, anticipating my needs for
affection and reassurance, encouraging me in the preparation for the birth of our son.

I chose from the maidservants a capable girl named
Keturah to become Isaac's nurse. Her early duties were to

make or to secure from the marketplace everything my baby would need. He should lack nothing. As she brought the items to me, I stored them as carefully as if they were jewels for a crown.

I wove two white wool blankets for my baby and worked into them designs of the flowers of Canaan.

As the Lord God had spoken, at the appointed time, our son was born, and we did name him Isaac, calling all who would ever hear of him to laugh with us because of the joy he brought to us—and, in God's mysterious way, to the people of the whole world as well.

It was indeed a time of laughter such as our camp had never known. Abraham called for a week of celebration. There was feasting, dancing, singing—and very long sessions around campfires where our servants crowded in to hear Abraham speak. He was eloquent as he talked of his God who created the world, then destroyed it, then remade it—who now had chosen a people through whom He would work for as long as the renewed world lasted. He impressed on them the part they had in this and encouraged them to believe in and worship only the one true God, El Elyon, El Shaddai. He had not spoken this strongly since the early days on the route from Ur to Haran. He had more than regained his first devoted enthusiasm to his God!

Isaac was a testimony to the power of the Lord and to the certainty of His promises. As our people watched him grow, they constantly would be reminded of our God.

He was all I dreamed my baby would be. Holding him close, I held my reason for being! Feeling his soft, small body against mine as I nursed him, touching his tiny fingers and letting them grasp my finger, hearing his first cries, and seeing his early smiles were causes for a quiet bliss I could not begin to explain to anyone else. Even when he would grow up and away from my constant care, these indelible moments would always be mine to enjoy forever!

Abraham was fortunate to have dependable servants

who did not need much overseeing so he could be occupied primarily with being near Isaac. He seldom left our tent in those next few weeks for more than two or three hours at a time.

I think Abraham and I had never really been happy before! Like most parents, we concluded that ours was the most beautiful child ever born. Never such eyes as his had opened on this world! He seemed to grow just fast enough and strong enough to be perfect for his age, and no baby could have ever evidenced such intelligence at so tender an age! Our Friend had given him the ideal name, for Isaac did mean laughter for us—unrestrained, merry, from-the-heart laughter! Our life had been enriched beyond all expectation.

Abraham's love for Ishmael had not lessened with the birth of his second son, but the time he spent with him decreased rapidly. The natural attention all babies get would seem unnatural to Ishmael—I was certain of that. Would he show his jealousy? I hoped not, for I wanted Abraham to have no cloud on his present joy.

Although many of our servants had stopped by to see Isaac at one time or another and to tell us how beautiful he was, neither Hagar nor Ishmael had come near. Their absence was so noticeable it seemed like an ominous presence. Thoughts of them crept into my mind more often than I should have liked.

Keturah and I took Isaac for walks, in part to have him enjoy the outdoors, and in part to show off our handsome boy who was soon to be a whole year old.

On the anniversary of his birth Abraham went into Gerar, saying there was a caravan due in from Damascus. He wanted to meet it and would bring me a fine present. He had brought so many gifts before Isaac was born, I surely didn't need another, but I was happy that he wanted to please me and to mark this day as special.

He returned so early that I knew there could not have been time to bargain over prices—hardly time to look over the wares the caravan brought in. I decided he must have changed his mind about selecting a gift for me. But he was carrying something—a small chest.

"It came, Sarah, just as I had ordered it a few months ago. Here—for a gown for Isaac's mother."

I opened it, loving the suspense of what it would be. With happy amazement I saw it was of heavy white silk, lavishly embroidered. I touched it to my face, smoothed it with my hand, then tossed some of the lustrous fabric over my shoulder as an improvised tunic. I was imagining how it would look when it was made up and what a great dinner party I would have to give in order to wear it for others to see. It was made to be seen!

As I stood admiring Abraham's gift, I saw him almost shyly take a very small cedar box he had been holding and place in on the table beside me. He helped me fold the silk back into its place then motioned to the box. "This is for my princess. Open it!"

In the box was the most magnificent bracelet I had ever seen. There were 12 jewels, each different from the other, each a perfect circle, and each set in the carved circlet of gold.

"I had it made especially for you, Sarah. It holds the colors of the land of Canaan. The mother of the people to whom God has given this land will be remembered and honored by all their generations and beyond them, by those of other nations who will be blessed by our descendants. This should have been a crown, my princess, but a bracelet will have to do."

He took my hand and slipped the exquisite piece of jewelry onto my wrist. I stared at it, spellbound. I turned it slowly, looking long into each stone before concentrating on the next one.

"Abraham, oh, Abraham!" I ransacked my vocabulary

frantically to find a proper word to tell him what it meant to me, how beautiful it was.

He must have accepted my stammering as the highest praise and deepest appreciation. He tossed his head back and laughed heartily at his speechless wife before he took me into his arms. He held me for a long while, until a mounting cry from our more precious treasure called me back to the every-day ecstasy of attending to Isaac. When I picked him up, his eye was caught by the glitter on my arm. He reached out a chubby hand to touch it and prattled something like, "OOooah!" He was as fluent as I had been — and apparently liked the bracelet as much!

My bracelet became almost part of me; I wore it every day. It increased in dearness as I saw it did hold, as Abraham suggested so poetically, the colors of our land.

I named them all:

    White jasper — like the snows of Mt. Hermon

    Sapphire — the vibrant blue of Kinnereth's Sea

    Chalcedony — mingled blues and whites like the
        splashing surf of the Great Sea

    Emerald — as green as Canaan's pasturelands

    Sardonyx — brown mated with gold like the fertile
        soil and ripening grain

    Carnelian — the happy looking red of wild tulips

    Chrysolite — yellow-tinged green of olives, not
        yet ripe

    Beryl — the shimmering shade of blue-green
        Lake Huleh

    Topaz — a sparkling chip of Canaan's autumn-
        hazed sunlight

    Chrysoprase — matching early shoots of almond
        leaves

    Jacinth — swirling tints of red, orange, yellow and

>   violet like a miniature of the hill country's
>   flowered carpet in the early spring
> Amethyst — crystalized purple of Canaan's
>   marvelous grapes.
> My favorite stone? Each one!

I saw reflected in the lovely facets of this flawless orna-ment Canaan's seas and lakes, its mountains and hills, its pasturelands and rich fields, its crops and trees, and its abundantly wild profusion of bright flowers. It was a glis-tening talisman, circle-shaped to symbolize the endless covenant.

Our next two years were peaceful ones. With the help of Keturah I cared for Isaac. Abraham saw to the herdsmen and the trading caravans sent out from our camp. We both worshiped at the altar each day, and from time to time Abraham offered up sacrifices to our God. Abraham was a beloved priest and wise counsellor to our servants and their families. He spent generous amounts of time with them when they needed his guidance.

The miracle of the birth of our son never lost its wonder for us. We could never have loved him so much if we had not waited for him so long.

...it is through Isaac that your offspring will be reckoned.
Genesis 21:12

*A*braham saw Ishmael less often now. There were no more long jaunts for the two of them, less hunting for deer and ibex, few trips into Gerar.

One day when he was disappointed by the postponement of a hunting trip, I heard an angry Ishmael say, "Now that you have another son, I am not your son!"

Abraham was jolted by the boy's fiery jealousy. "Ishmael, you will always be my son. Ishmael, listen to me! You are cared for and well provided for, and you are loved.

"I am older now than when you were a little boy, and it is taking me longer to get my work done. Also it seems more time is needed with all the servants, helping them with their problems and talking to them about our faithful God. The neighboring herdsmen come over more often now to chat with me for long hours. And . . . there is Isaac. You are still my son, Ishmael, but so is Isaac. You must allow me to spend time with him and with these others I have mentioned as I think it proper."

Ishmael scowled, turned abruptly from Abraham and ran to where he had tied his camel. He loosened him, mounted up, and rode out across the grazing land without looking back at his father. The next time Abraham tried to arrange with him for a hunting trip, he refused to go.

The day came for Isaac to be weaned. This traditionally

was an important family celebration, and Abraham pro-
claimed a great feast day in honor of the occasion.
Invitations were sent to neighboring herdsmen, merchants
and townspeople in Gerar. A messenger was even dis-
patched to Hebron to ask Ephron and his wife to help us
rejoice in our beloved son.

Isaac, loved and fussed over every day, was on this
particular day praised, given gifts, and generally smiled
upon by all our guests. He was the center of attention.

Ishmael, who had become more wild and undisciplined
in the past months, began to edge his way to the place where
Isaac played. He stared at my little one in contempt and then
started to imitate his childish speech. His imitation brought
nervous laughter from our guests. Then he began to imitate
them. He mocked the way they complimented Isaac and the
way I had received the compliments. He imitated Abraham
speaking of God's great miracle here in our midst.

The day we had thought would be one of the best in
our life was being turned into a nightmare. No one could
silence Ishmael. Hagar stood at the edge of the crowd,
obviously pleased with the dashing flair of her son. She
made no attempt to stop his vicious ridiculing of our family
and friends.

Our guests were understandably confused. There was a
tenseness in the air that overcame any attempt to maintain
the attitude of celebration.

We got through the day, and I was thankful that our
visitors were perceptive enough to take early leave.

"Abraham! Send this slavewoman and her son away!
Ishmael will not be heir with my son Isaac!" I had been
choking back frustration and embarrassment while we had
guests, but now that we were alone I indulged in hysterics.

"On this special day, to be so grieved in my heart..."
Abraham said it over and over as he sat with his head buried
in his hands, his elbows resting on his knees.

"Send them away!"

"Sarah," he looked at me through tears. "Ishmael is my son. I love him. I have a duty to raise him. I want him here."

"Send them away!"

"Ishmael will outgrow this rebellious age. I have not spent enough time with him, have not kept him busy enough. I will give him flocks to herd, make him feel grown up, make him feel he has not been replaced in my affection by Isaac. He will change. Give the boy time."

"SEND THEM AWAY!"

There were no more words between us that night and by morning I had more mellow thoughts about it all.

"Abraham, my feelings were shouting at you last night because of the way Ishmael ruined the day I had looked forward to for such a long time. It is not reason to turn them out. I am sorry."

"I am sending them away." Abraham raised his arm to signal to me that I must not interrupt with any arguments. "I am not sending them away because of a ruined celebration, or because of personality clashes that are inevitable. I have known since before Isaac was born that I must send them away. If I had already done it, we would have been spared that dreadful experience yesterday."

Abraham had lowered his arm, and I was not so intimidated as to keep still. "What reason would you have for sending them away besides our clashes with them from time to time? If they would just change their attitudes—and last night you said Ishmael would change—perhaps they can stay. After all, where would they go? I was not being realistic last night; I was not even trying to be kind."

Abraham stood up. He seemed to tower six inches taller when he was angry. "Don't make it harder for me to do what I must do. You help me more when you shout 'Send them away!' This, as I have told you, is what I must do.

"Remember the things I told you about my meeting with our God when He gave us new names and promised Isaac's birth would be within one year?"

"Of course I remember! But that had nothing to do with Ishmael and Hagar. It had to do only with us."

"It also had to do with them, but I did not tell you that part. When God assured me of a son by my beloved wife, I begged Him that Ishmael also might be blessed as my son. I said to Him, 'If only Ishmael might live under your blessing!'

"In answer to that prayer God said he would bless Ishmael. He would become the father of another nation of twelve princes. But his original choice was unalterable. The covenant people will not be Ishmael's, but Isaac's. We must be separate from Ishmael and his nation."

Abraham stared at the ceiling for some time, as if waiting for God to intervene. Finally he continued, almost talking to himself but aware I was listening.

"I have not sent them away sooner because I found it too difficult. Now it is plain that I have waited too long. I have allowed the situation to get out of hand to the point where it has brought heartache to us, embarrassment to our friends, and—I am certain—grief to our God."

Abraham was sobbing. He cried with the sharp grief of sending his oldest son away. He cried with the heavy remorse of not having obeyed his God promptly.

"My tears are even in disobedience." Abraham quieted himself and looked to me for comfort which I did not know how to give.

"Is grief the same as disobedience, my husband?"

"This time it is, for I have been commanded to do this willingly. Last night I did not go to the place of the altar, but my Lord came to me. He said, 'Do not be so distressed about the boy and your maidservant. Listen to what Sarah tells you, because it is through Isaac that your offspring will be reckoned.'"

He needed no more words from me. He only needed the memory of El Shaddai's telling him that even against natural emotions he must learn to put the grief away.

I brought him a pitcher of milk, some bread, and clusters of grapes for his breakfast. He looked at the food for a moment then rose quickly to his feet, and with long, decisive strides he left the tent. I saw him cross to the path that led to Ishmael's and Hagar's tent. I felt no sense of personal victory in what was to come.

He returned shortly, telling me he would be waiting on the Lord in the holy place of meeting for the rest of the day. I should not wait up for him, for he would be gone until his inner turmoil had been calmed.

The scene with Ishmael and Hagar had drained him emotionally. He looked desolate. He needed to be comforted and renewed and strengthened to do what had to be done only by his God.

I heard him come to bed late that night. I got up a few minutes later to see if he wanted to talk; he already was sleeping. I knew he had been ministered to by his enabling God.

He arose early the next morning. I was already awake and went out to talk with him. He only wanted quiet, and, kissing me gently, he went out to meet for the last time in his life his cherished firstborn and the woman who was his mother.

When he came back, he continued his silence, but it was too painful. I had to end it—even if he was not ready.

"They have gone?"

"Yes."

"Did you give them provisions? Did they have camels and attendants?"

"No camels, no attendants. I gave them a skin of water and some bread. But more than this, I gave them the direct absolute word of God that He would provide for them and would bring His promises to Ishmael into reality. I told them this was God's expressed command for them—that they should go, and that as they went they should trust completely in His constant care."

"Do they believe God will protect them, prosper them?"

"Perhaps. Hagar remembers the time the angel of the Lord appeared to her in another time of great need, directing her to safety and comfort. With that experience in her memory she can think positively—to some degree—about His immediate and future plans for her son and herself."

"Were they angry?"

"More defiant than angry."

"Abraham, I . . ."

"There are no words that can change things, or soften things. Let us give up speaking of Ishmael and Hagar as we have now given up their companionship. They are gone.

"We are here, and we have much to live for."

23

Abraham planted a tamarisk tree in Beersheba, and there he called upon the name of the Lord, the Eternal God.   *Genesis 21:33*

*A*braham's attention was diverted quickly from his personal grief over Ishmael. There was serious trouble at an essential well on our grazing land. It had been taken from our shepherds by Abimelech's armed men, and there was the potential of greater violence. Determined to prevent further confrontation, but to have the well available again immediately, Abraham arranged an emergency meeting with Abimelech and his ministers.

Eliezer and Neri rode with Abraham to the well site where the king and his attendants had agreed to be. All three men were grim-faced as they left the camp. They meant to have that well back!

When they came home at the end of the day they were laughing and looked so relaxed in their saddles that it was easy to interpret how the meeting had gone.

"You don't have to tell me, Abraham. From half a mile away I could read your face and it said 'Good news!'"

"Half a mile—really?"

"...Well, half of that perhaps. From quite a distance, anyway. Did I read the message correctly?"

"Yes! I do have good news. Things went better than I could have hoped. Abimelech came in a mood of friendship and, given the explanation of the damage done by his servants, he claimed he hadn't known about it at all. We made suitable agreements—agreements that will protect even future generations.

"We named the place of the well Beersheba. There we both swore to keep our newly made contract. I will have my men plant a grove of tamarisk trees at the well to further permanently identify it. And, of course, at this grove of trees I will build a new altar of field stone.

"Sarah, every time I build a new altar I am, in the best way I know, claiming the land in the name of God. I praise and thank him that this matter with Abimelech was settled peacefully. Tomorrow I will wait before Him at the altar I will build at Beersheba."

Abraham went with his men the next morning to help plant the trees. He stayed behind when they came back to camp, and he had hours of sweet communion with God. The sun was setting when he came home, sending an orange-red glow over the landscape. It gave a few moments of magnificent glory to everything. Even the air seemed to be iridescent. That accounted for part of the radiance on Abraham's face—but only a small part.

He rushed to me, took hold of both my hands, and held them tight, smiling as only the bearer of good tidings can smile.

"You read my face yesterday, Sarah. What do you see there today?"

"That you have felt the close presence of our God."

"Yes. And we have a new name for Him. Remember when we only called Him the one God? Then the joy to hear Him called El Elyon, God Most High, by Melchizedek? When He was to display His mighty power to circumvent His own laws of nature and allow Isaac to be born to a woman past the age for that, He became known to us as El Shaddai, God Almighty. Each time we learn a new name for Him, we know Him better. Today another marvelous name is revealed. It is El Olam, the Everlasting God, signifying another facet of His character.

"Everlasting—that is a word to ponder! It makes days,

years, even a lifetime, seem so short. I suppose it is a word never fully comprehended, but one that helps us express the wonders of our God."

The next years at Gerar-Beersheba were years of comfort, filled with productive work for everyone in our camp. Flocks increased; the wool was plentiful; the spinners and the weavers worked diligently; our gardens were bountiful. Best of all, we had these placid years to watch our son grow strong and tall, wise and personable, devoutly worshiping El Olam.

Abraham again had the joy of teaching a son to ride, to hunt, to know and love the land. In addition, as Isaac reached young manhood, Abraham taught him how to herd sheep, how to outfit a caravan, how to plant and reap crops, and how to bargain with merchants and traders. But most of all—he taught Isaac of God. Isaac learned the carefully transmitted history of the race from Adam to his own time. He was impressed by the fact that he was a descendent of Shem. Shem's father, Noah, had been called out, as a man of faith in whom God was pleased, to restore and replenish the whole world after the deluge. Abraham had been called out as a man of faith from Ur to go to Canaan and establish a line of people to be a blessing for that same world. Isaac believed he and his forefather, Shem, had been blessed with two of the best fathers who ever lived.

One evening as Isaac, Abraham, and I sat around a family campfire, Isaac told us he had a question that had been bothering him for some time, but he didn't want us to be offended by it. Abraham encouraged him to speak. Whatever it was—even if we could not answer it—we would not be offended.

"All right then, here is my problem. It is impossible for me to understand how just living here in Canaan, being a herdsman-merchant-farmer, and worshiping the one God is going to be more than just that. Of course, that is quite enough for a fine life. But how is it going to affect the world?"

Abraham understood the boy's strong desire for a dramatic, rapid unfolding of events. He had experienced the same feeling when he was young. It had made him impatient with everything, including himself. Even now he wished he had an answer that would be satisfying to Isaac—and to the young man of Ur who still lived in his memory. He could tell only what he had learned over the years in many difficult lessons. I knew Abraham would choose his words carefully, and he did.

"God has not fully revealed it to me, but I have had a glimpse of a long, troubled future. He showed it to me the day of the covenant ritual. I saw down through the ages the upheavals, the wars, and other disasters that our people must endure. I saw down through a long tunnel of years to a time when one from our line will come and will be the one to work out God's plan to completion. Meanwhile, it is important that we never underestimate the importance of both waiting to learn His will, and then doing it. We can then entrust the next generation with the line of promise.

"Isaac, you are the key person in the next generation. You must stay faithful to God, instructing your children to do the same for through one of them this line will be extended.

"It is difficult at times—this life of faith. It is easy to be tempted away from it by others, by your own inclinations, even by your own...common sense. You must learn the value of daily waiting on the Lord, even on days when it seems you can't ever hope to see His face or feel His presence—waiting, trusting, and obeying immediately what you clearly know is His will."

"It sounds too easy, father."

"That is because you have not yet really tried it, my son."

Over those precious years Abraham led Isaac, by words and example, to a solid faith in God. Isaac went with him regularly to pray at the altar and to help when Abraham selected the best lamb from the flocks and prepared it for sacrifice.

Each year I loved the land more; each season, in turn, became my favorite. We had an olive grove in the east section of our acreage—huge trunks gnarled in fascinating shapes, leaves wearing a lovely grey-green color. Olive trees never die. Even if one is cut down, new shoots come up from roots of the old one. I would have liked olive trees just for their beauty. But they were more than ornamental, providing oil for cooking and for some of the medications we needed. And of course the olives themselves were a tasty part of our diet. The harvest of olives came late in September. Isaac helped beat the trees, gather the fruit, put it into tall baskets, and take it to the olive press.

After the winter rains in late October the wheat and barley would be planted. The men made furrows with bronze tipped wooden plows, and the women scattered the seed in the furrows.

First harvest was in the spring—our busiest time. There was flax to be cut, dried, then spun into fiber. There was barley to be harvested next, and then wheat. The field workers kept flint edged sickles busy for many hours each day. Women who did not help in the field prepared big meals for the workers who came in from the harvest with enormous appetites.

After reaping the grain came the tedious work of separating it from the stalks and then from the chaff. It was taken to the community threshing floor, winnowed, and at last stored in large earthenware containers for use in the months ahead. Many times our crops were so bountiful that old Zaccar could go into Gerar with a good amount to sell.

Abraham had large areas planted in gardens which were tended and harvested all through the spring, summer, and fall. Like the olive trees, they combined beauty and utility—lettuce, sea holly, parsley, chickory, beans, lentils, garlic, leeks, cucumbers, onions, and chickpeas in fine rows. We had a few fig and pomegranate trees. Eye-pleasing, mouth-watering fruit filled their lovely branches.

One especially large job was the grape harvest. We ate grapes fresh from the vine; we dried many to use in the winter; and we made most of them into wine.

In both spring and fall, during the migrations of quail, Abraham and Isaac and some of our servants bagged many for special feasts. They also occasionally brought in rock partridges.

Isaac grew more handsome each year. He was amiable to friends and servants; he was obedient to his father and me; he was devoted to his God. No parents ever were more pleased with their son than we were.

"Abraham, our Isaac is a fine young man—the finest!"

"There has never been one day of his life I have not thanked God for him, and it seems each day Isaac gives us more reasons to be thankful."

My mind latched onto an incredible thought. I shared it with Abraham with a self-deprecating laugh, for it was so wild that I would not want him to guess I was serious about it. "Once I thought if only I could live long enough to see Issac grown to manhood, I would be satisfied. But now that I have done this, I hope for still more. I would like to live to see my grandchild!"

He did not laugh at me; he only looked dumbfounded! But since he had not laughed, I pressed the point and asked, "Do you think this might be possible?"

Then the laughter came—a sweet, amused laughter tempered with words to answer my question and yet spare my feelings. "I don't know, Sarah. But I do know it is always good to have a reason to want to live on in this good land, and it is pleasant to think about grandchildren."

And so we would sit and talk about things, lovely things like—sometimes—grandchildren.

It was early spring. There was a splendid sky—a lovely

moon serenely shining while small, teasing, opaque clouds drifted across it creating varying shades of darkness and light.

"Isaac has not seen all of the land yet, Abraham. You should take him on a trip. Let him see Mt. Tabor, Mts. Ebal and Gerizim, Mt. Carmel, the Sea of Kinnereth and Lake Huleh, Bethel and Ai, Jericho and Hebron, the Salt Sea and the Negev, the Great Sea and the road that winds up the coast and over to Megiddo. He has never seen these places, and he should see them all. And when you take him on this journey, don't tell him only of the history of each place and its commercial value. Remind him also to look at the display of flowers, from the peonies in the mountains to the lilies in the fields around Kinnereth and along the Jordan. Call his attention to the variety of birds that add their music and color to his land. He must look at everything, not as a chance traveler might who just wants to get across it to the cities of Egypt or the Chaldeans. He must see the land as a God-given legacy for him and his descendents—forever."

"You are planning quite a trip! But you talk as though only Isaac and I will be going. Won't you be coming with us, if we do go on such a journey? You make it sound so interesting that I want to begin planning for it today yet. I wish we could start tomorrow morning!"

"I am glad you like the idea enough to be impatient to get it worked out. I have thought of this trip for a long time and have enjoyed it as I pictured Isaac's delight at seeing the pleasant, fruitful, glorious land God has chosen for His people. But dreaming about travel is one thing; actually going is another. Perhaps you and Issac could go without me for I hardly feel strong enough to try it."

"I would not enjoy the trip without you."

"You must enjoy it—twice as much—so you can enjoy it for me, too. And then you can come back and tell me all about it."

"Sarah, my princess, you have a way of making the

illogical sound almost rational. All right, I will try to enjoy it for you. I am so glad you thought of such a good thing for Issac."

Abraham stood up, stretched his arms high above his head, took a deep breath, and said, "Life is good, and it is getting richer, deeper in meaning all the time. I am going to find Isaac yet tonight and tell him to start planning for a long, happy tour of inspection of his inheritance. He will be even more excited about it than I am, but he will want you to be with us."

"Tell him . . . tell him I will be seeing the two of you in my mind as you go, thinking of you all the time, and seeing in my memories all the places you are seeing, but without the discomfort of travel."

The thought of my husband and my son going without me was not pleasant, but I would not have it seem to them that I was bothered by it. I could not pretend to myself that I had the stamina such a venture would require of me. It would be nice, though, if I could see Mamre again, with its massive oak trees that seemed to have the permanence of the olive trees.

"Moonlight,"—since Abraham had gone to find Isaac, I just talked to the moon—"keep shining each night on my dear ones while they are away from me."

It would have been fun to have heard Abraham tell Isaac of the spontaneously planned trip. With Isaac's youthful enthusiasm he would hurry Abraham into leaving as soon as possible. That night I drifted off easily to sleep, hoping they soon could organize things at the camp, then pack and be on their way.

Abraham did not come to bed at all that night. Early the next morning, before full daylight, I heard muffled, excited voices outside in the direction of the road. I got up to see what was happening. Abraham, Issac, Eliezer, and two servants were preparing a small pack train. It was nothing like the one they would need for the journey we had been talking about. From the sound of their voices and the glimpse I had of Abraham as he talked to Eliezer, I could see that he did not look like one about to go on a pleasant pilgrimage. There was something about his face that chilled me through and through. I was unable to call out to ask what he was doing, where he was going, why he had not come to say good-bye before he and Isaac left, or what route they would take. Nothing about the scene seemed real.

Abraham was saying to Eliezer, "We should be back within a week. Tell Sarah there was unexpected business to attend to. Ask her not to be anxious about us, but to pray. I cannot tell you the exact place we are going, but it is in the land of Moriah, near Salem. God has promised to lead us to a mountain of his choosing there. He will be with us, and all will be well."

24

Early the next morning Abraham got up and saddled his donkey. He took with him two of his servants and his son Isaac. When he had cut enough wood for the burnt offering, he set out for the place God had told him about.   *Genesis 22:3*

*F*or the first time Abraham had not confided in me about his plans. Something was very wrong, but I had no idea what it was.

Where were they going? What were they going to do? Why could Abraham not have told me about it? The anxiety of not knowing something can be almost as unsettling as facing whatever it is!

They each had taken one attendant. They could have had clothing and food for only a few days in so small a pack train. There was a supply of wood strapped to one of the donkeys, and I saw Abraham hand to one of his young men the pan he used for the hot coals in the sacrifice ritual.

Was he going to build an altar somewhere? If so, why was he not looking joyful and eager to get on with it as he had at Bethel, Mamre, and Beersheba?

If the place for the altar was a two- or three-day journey away, why was the sacrificial animal not taken along with their baggage? I had not seen any. It would be too far to come back to get it, and Abraham never would buy some-one else's lamb for an offering. The lambs he chose were always the most excellent from all his herds. He would single out the sacrificial lamb days in advance, when possible, to watch it carefully to be sure it had no defects before offering it to God. Only the choicest lamb for God!

The thoughts that hurtled into my mind were the essence of mystery, wild and terrible. I ran from the tent to the now empty road leading away from camp, and I screamed, "Abraham! You didn't take the lamb!"

I sat down by the side of the road, but I could no longer see it because of the tears that had filled my eyes. To an empty, blurry landscape—to a husband who was no longer within hearing—I cried, "Abraham! You didn't take the lamb! You left so early this morning that you weren't really awake! You remembered to take food and clothing. You had an attendant for yourself and one for Isaac. You took a pan to carry the hot embers to the altar. You took the wood for the fire. You took Isaac...but...you did not take the lamb!"

Again my voice rose to a scream, "You took Isaac! You took—ISAAC!"

My body shook from the cool of the morning and from the chilling thought in my mind, the thing I knew but would not yet admit, even to myself. At that precise moment I felt overwhelmed by a sensation of warm, liquid love overcoming the cold and the fear inside me, infusing me with calmness and strength. I knew El Shaddai had come to me in my bitterest hour.

I went back to the tent, pulled a shawl around me and sat down to what I knew would be a long vigil.

Taunting, stinging, hornet-like questions darted at me—questions for which I had no answer. I needed to keep my mind occupied with other thoughts. I centered them on God Himself and tried to remember all the things He had ever promised Abraham and me and Isaac. I said His wonderful names over and over and praised Him for being holy, omnipotent, and everlasting—and our Friend.

My days and nights ran together in a mixture of praying and praising God. I pushed recurring thoughts of horror from my mind by saying again—and claiming again—His promises. I scarcely ate anything. I slept only slightly. Part of the time I was in a state of semiconsciousness.

When they had been gone five days, I remembered Abraham's olive-wood box. God's words were written on the papyrus inside. I could not read them, but I knew many of them by heart, and the box was something tangible to hold in my empty hands.

I pushed aside a large wicker chest, lifted the mat it had rested on, dug down into the earth beneath, and brought out a copper box. Inside was the linen-wrapped olive-wood box that held the writings. I gently took away the wrappings, lifted the lid of the box, and touched the thin pages. Then I carried the box back to where I was keeping my vigil, ready to protect it with my life.

I prayed again, now with more confidence. I called on El Shaddai, who made life come from a dead womb, to send Abraham back to me quickly with our son! The boldness of the prayer startled me, but I prayed it again. Then I prayed His own words back to Him, "Is anything too hard for the Lord?"

At last I was content to be quiet before Him, as Abraham had learned to be so long ago. Later in the afternoon I noticed another olive-wood box that had been stored between the folds of blankets on a low shelf. In it were my trinkets from Ur. I smiled to think how important the things in it once were to me. I stared at it in some amusement, holding Abraham's box against my heart in joy that to anyone else would have seemed inappropriate or insane at such a time as this!

I thought about the records in the box, not only those of our immediate family, but those of the earliest fathers, carefully handed down over many generations. My mind finally went back to Eve. I had never thought much about her before, but now I suddenly had great sympathy for this woman whose one son killed another. She must have experienced intolerable trouble and grief. She lived to have more sons and daughters. Her son Seth was the beginning of the line that culminated in Noah. I suppose her other children eased her hurt somewhat, but they could not erase the scars.

There would be no more children for me. Even as I thought that, I remembered He really could, if He wanted to, have me bear a dozen more children! But He would have no need for that. He had promised that through Isaac our line would be reckoned. And there would be only one Isaac.

Isaac! I prayed one more time, "My God, I believe you have Isaac in your care. Help my faith to be as strong as my words."

It was dark now. Before going to bed I went out to look at the stars which had become God-given symbols of the multitude of our descendants. Clouds had moved in, and there was not a star to be seen. But they were there! It took no great faith to believe the stars were still there, even though I could not see them. I opened my arms to the skies and thanked God for the unseen stars!

Abraham had told Eliezer the trip would take about seven days. It had already been six days. I knew I must sleep long and well that night for Abraham would be coming in the morning. Abraham and Isaac would be coming in the morning, and I wanted to be at my best. I closed my eyes, called up a picture of stars and counted them determinedly until I fell into a deep, untroubled sleep.

I was awakened in the dawn light by shouting. The guard Eliezer had posted on the road to watch for Abraham and his small pack train had run into the center of the camp, rousing everyone with the news that the master was returning.

I breathed the strengthening names of my God, then hurriedly dressed. Not since he had come back from the war with Kedorlaomer was I so eager to see him. And I was eager to see....

Suddenly he was in the door of the tent, holding out his arms to me. Reading my mixed emotions of fear-tinged joy, he encircled me with one arm and with the other he waved to some one outside. "Come on in Isaac. Your mother wants to see you."

Three people embraced—three people who never would take life for granted again—three people who would think often of the past six days of the things each had learned about themselves, each other, and God.

When emotions subsided enough for speech we sat down to hear Abraham begin telling of all that had happened.

"God came to me the night I left you to go tell Isaac of our proposed trip, Sarah. He had a terrifyingly different kind of trip in mind for us. I was walking through the cool, moonlit evening when I heard Him call my name. I answered, 'Here I am.'"

"And He said, 'Take your son, your only son, Isaac, whom you love, and go to the region of Moriah. Sacrifice him there as a burnt offering on one of the mountains I will tell you about.'"

Abraham put a rough right hand over his mouth and let his thumb and forefinger dab at a tear glistening in each eye. "I will spare you both my own thoughts and feelings about this. Each one of us is too emotionally drained at the moment for the telling or the hearing of the turmoil I suffered as I struggled to make the necessary preparations.

"Since there was no mistaking either God's voice or His instructions, I decided that delayed obedience would have been even more difficult than swift obedience. To have had to think about what I had to do for even one extra hour would have intensified the crushing burden of it.

"I paced through the camp for a long time as I tried to collect my thoughts about how to proceed. Then I went to alert Isaac and our servants, Zuar and Helon, that we would be traveling to a new location for an altar in the morning, and that we would be traveling light.

"I went back to the tent and tried to sleep, but it was impossible. I prayed, hoping different instructions would come from God, making the trip unnecessary. None came. I arose early in the morning and saddled my donkey. I took the two young servants and Isaac to cut the wood for the burnt offering. We packed it on the animals along with other necessary things.

"I thought of several different ways to come to you, Sarah, and tell you what we were doing, but each way sounded so very harsh that I wanted to spare you from hearing it. I knew you would be upset at my not talking with you before I left. I saw you standing at the door of the tent but pretended not to notice. I kept hoping you would not come out to where we were, for I could not face you with the awfulness of it all.

"As we all started down the road, God told me the exact place we should go—Mt. Moriah, near Salem.

"Early on the third day out I saw the hill from a distance. As we came closer, I could see rugged limestone outcroppings protruding from its sides, forming bulges and indentations of grotesque shapes. Some of these rocks, on the east side of the hill, resembled the outline of a skull.

"I halted our group at the base of the hill and told the young men to wait with the animals while my son and I went up on the mountain to worship.

"I told them we would come back to them shortly. It was a simple sentence, but it made my voice tremble. It was my statement of faith in God Most High who had entered into an agreement with me concerning this son and his descendants. His word could not be broken or revoked, no matter what the circumstances appeared to be. I chose to believe in a truth that contradicted what seemed to be happening.

"I took the wood for the burnt offering and laid it on Isaac's back. I carried the pan of hot embers and the knife. We began to climb the hill together."

In spite of his desire to keep strong emotions from surfacing during the telling, Abraham had been fighting for control. Now he gave way to quiet sobs as he remembered the moments he was describing.

Isaac's strong voice took up the account at this point. "I said to him, 'Father? The fire and wood are here, but where is the lamb for the burnt offering?'

"He told me without any hesitation, 'God himself will provide the lamb for the burnt offering, my son.'

"So we went to the exact spot God had told him of — a very large flat stone area. Father built an altar there and laid the wood in order. He looked at me, and I looked at him. There was no lamb, and then I understood the look of terror and grief on his face. I knew why his hand trembled as he motioned for me to lie down on the altar. I hoped he did not hear my heart as it pounded inside me. Facing such a death was frightening — but the incomprehensibility of it was even more terrifying! I suddenly felt cut off . . . from my father . . . from my God! Why? WHY! All my life I was taught I was to be God's link to the generation after me. What had I done to make Him angry? Did He know what was happening? Did He care? My unvoiced questions received no answers. I decided that what must be done should be done bravely by both my father and me.

"We had a short time of silent prayer, and then I allowed myself to be tied to the altar."

I had kept from interrupting their incredible narrative until then, but I heard myself saying, "Isaac, you had the strength to overpower your father and run. Did you try?"

"No. I had given myself up to death when I laid on the altar."

"Even after you were tied, you could have shouted to the waiting servants to come free you. Did you call?"

"No. In the time of prayer I just told you about, God impressed on my mind the necessity of absolute trust. I wanted to run — yes! I wanted to call for help — yes! But I willed to submit to this death."

Abraham had regained his voice and again took up the story of those moments of desolation. "I had it in my power to free him even though he did not try to evade his fate. I would so gladly have taken his place if it had been possible. To give my own life would have been far easier than to call up the strength to kill my well-beloved son.

"I raised the knife to plunge it as quickly as possible, knowing my own heart would break as the knife burst the heart of Isaac.

"And suddenly the angel of the Lord called out from heaven and said, 'Abraham!'"

My husband raised his head slightly, his eyes moist again with tears, his chin quivering. In a moment he continued, "He stopped my knife when it was past the point I could have stopped it myself!

"At that worst of all moments I was overshadowed with His love for both Isaac and me. And there was something else, another emotion mixed in with His love—it was a supernatural sadness so heavy you could feel its oppression—as if...as if the sacrifice we had just attempted stood for one that would be made later, one that would be finished."

"Involving Isaac again?"

"No, but involving one who will come from our line. And this dark, brooding sadness and overwhelming love of God will surround him on that day.

"After the angel stopped my hand, he said, 'Do not lay a hand on the boy. Do not do anything to him. Now I know that you fear God, because you have not withheld from me your son, your only son.'"

"And I looked up and there was a ram caught in a thicket by his horns. I went over and took the ram and offered it as a burnt offering...instead of my son."

The telling of the tumultous experience had eased the tensions we each had felt so keenly. We sat quietly, occupied with personal reaction to all that had been said and done.

Isaac began speaking again. "And my father called the name of that place 'The Lord will provide.'

"And then," Isaac's face looked like Abraham's the first time he had heard the voice of God. He stopped for a breath and then went on, "And then the angel of the Lord called out from heaven a second time and said, 'I swear by myself, declares the Lord, that because you have done this and have not withheld your son, your only son, I will surely bless you and make descendants as numerous as the stars in the sky and as the sand on the seashore. Your descendants will take possession of the cities of their enemies and through your offspring all nations on earth will be blessed, because you have obeyed me.'"

Abraham had been nodding his head in enraptured agreement as Isaac recalled the words of the angel of the Lord. Now he smiled and said, "Then I returned to the young men with Isaac, and we all came home.

"Sarah," he leaned toward me, suddenly solicitous about my own experience in these long days, "what did you think when we left with no explanation and stayed so long? Did you worry? Were you angry?"

"I want to tell you of my own experiences while you were away, but that will be for another time. Now we are all too tired for further talk. I will set out some bread and cheese, some fruit and wine. We will eat and then rest."

"My precious princess, you are right. We are tired. When we have eaten and rested, we will hear from you about your last few days. I know the presence of our God was with you, too.

"I see you have the box of papyrus out. You knew I would have much to write, and I do. But that also will have to wait until tomorrow."

25

By faith Abraham, when called to go to a place he would later receive as his inheritance, obeyed and went, even though he did not know where he was going. By faith he made his home in the promised land like a stranger in a foreign country; he lived in tents, as did Isaac and Jacob, who were heirs with him of the same promise. For he was looking forward to the city with foundations, whose architect and builder is God.

By faith Abraham, even through he was past age—and Sarah herself was barren—was enabled to become a father because he considered him faithful who had made the promise. And so from this one man, and he as good as dead, came descendants as numerous as the stars in the sky and as countless as the sand on the seashore.

All these people were living by faith when they died. They did not receive the things promised; they only saw them and welcomed them from a distance. And they admitted that they were aliens and strangers on earth. People who say such things show that they are looking for a country of their own. If they had been thinking of the country they had left, they would have had opportunity to return. Instead, they were longing for a better country—a heavenly one. Therefore God is not ashamed to be called their God, for he has prepared a city for them.   *Hebrews 11:8-16*

We welcomed the easy months after the return of the men from Mt. Moriah. Spring sparkled into summer; crops and herds flourished. It was time to harvest the grapes that hung in large, amethyst-colored clusters from their strong green vines.

"Sarah, I called you three times. Didn't you hear me?"

"No, I didn't hear you. I am sorry, Abraham. What do you want?"

"Nothing as important as whatever occupied your mind so totally that you didn't hear me call! What were you thinking about?"

"Oh—I was thinking—about one of my favorite places in Canaan."

"The Sea of Kinnereth? The shores of the Great Sea?"

"Oh, yes, those are favorites, too. But I was remembering Mamre. I would like to see those pleasant fields again, the wonderful oak trees, and the altar you built there. I believe I could travel that far. Do you think we might visit there sometime soon?"

"I will see about it, Sarah. I see no reason we cannot do it."

"Soon?"

"Yes, very soon. I will send a messenger to Ephron to find out how things are there now."

Weeks went by. The grapes were all gathered and were in the process of being dried for winter or made into wine. The late summer was exceptionally warm. Abraham said nothing more about Mamre.

We received word from Haran, mentioning family members we had never seen. It had been so long since we had been with Milcah and Nahor that we probably would not even recognize each other now, but it was good to hear from them. This brought distant days back to our minds. Abraham reminisced for hours about the times of caravaning, the days at Bethel, the breathtaking view of Kinnereth and its surrounding hills when we first saw it one golden day soon after we had crossed into Canaan.

By encouraging me to think along those lines, Abraham had been leading up to the topic he wanted to talk about. He cleared his throat and said quite casually, "By the way, Sarah, talking about all these old days reminds me of something you said a few days ago. Do you, by any chance, still care about going to Mamre?"

"Oh, yes! I thought you had forgotten all about it. We haven't talked of it since that afternoon several weeks ago—weeks, not days, Abraham. Maybe months, I don't know. Anyway, I was certain you had decided against it or forgotten."

"I did not forget, and I have been working on a surprise for you. We are going back to Mamre to stay. I have been in touch with Ephron, and he has plenty of fields for us to rent again. We can have the same ones we had before, plus additional acreage with a substantial number of olive trees on it and an extra well. We should be there within a month, for I have already begun the work of breaking camp here."

"Abraham, that is the most wonderful surprise you could have given me. I have enjoyed the years here at Gerar, but Mamre still seems more like home.

"Won't moving so large a camp as ours be a terribly difficult undertaking? Are you sure you want to do it? We have so much more to move now! Just a trip back to Mamre would be fine. We don't have to move."

"It is an excellent idea to move. That is one phase of Isaac's training I have not covered. He should know how to organize a move, how to secure grazing areas in another section of the land, how to handle the problems of a caravan, and how to set up camp again. Beside that, I love Mamre, too, and I look forward to being back where I can have those weekly visits with my good old friend, Ephron."

The journey back up into the highlands was a great accomplishment, for now we had thousands of animals and several hundred servants. Our household possessions had increased and, of course, so had the number of our tents. We required many oxcarts and pack animals. We still used porters; some of them were the strong, able descendants of the Luristan porters that had been with us when we left Ur.

The distance was not great between Gerar and Hebron, but to me it was like going to a different country. I loved the hills, the variety of trees—especially the oaks—and the cooler weather. And I loved Abraham for bringing me back to it all.

Abraham enjoyed the change too, and he lost no time in

renewing the weekly trips to Hebron to visit with Ephron.

We had been back at Mamre for two years. I was 127 years old. They had been two of the best years of my life. Loved by a faithful husband, comforted by a loving son, surrounded by faithful servants in a bountiful land—blessed by God.

The days had been getting away from me lately. I could not remember what I had done, if I had done anything. Had I tended to that little girl with a fever? Had I finished the green and blue mat for Isaac's tent?

I needed a lot of sleep and found it frustrating to be letting so many hours be taken from me in that seemingly useless way. All my cooking and other household chores were done by servants now, and I didn't mind a bit.

Abraham stayed busy—too busy. I wanted him beside me all the time, but I understood that could not be. Isaac worked by his father's side, learning more about the management of everything and becoming more knowledgeable about the legacy of the writings. He stopped in to see me nearly every day.

One morning I told them both that I would be too busy for the next few days to see them or talk with them. I had an important project to work on. I wanted to be left alone.

I didn't tell them what the project was, but it was to fulfill a great desire to review, uninterruptedly, my long life—in as much detail as possible.

These past few days I have been doing that, and it has been a remarkable experience. Memories crowded in on my mind so vividly that I could remember actual conversations. I remembered especially beautiful sights and recalled how I had reacted to the crises that kept bursting into my earlier life. Now it is finished, and I have sent for Abraham to come to me when it is convenient for him. I have missed him.

"You have kept me mystified, Sarah, for too long. What have you been doing? Your maidservant kept telling me only that your project would take a while—that you were not yet finished—that you were getting along well and would let me know when you could talk with me. What has this all been about? I cannot imagine!"

"I am sorry if I caused you any anxiety, Abraham. I suppose it was a silly thing anyway. I wanted to review my life—slowly and objectively. I wanted to pray for forgiveness for the wrong things, praise God for the good things, and—just see who I was and who I had become."

"Sarah, that is exciting. It is not silly and...."

"And—I am not finished speaking, Abraham—there are many things I would have done differently if I had been able to get my perspectives straight and my faith had been firmed up earlier....

"There are also happy...glorious times I treasure so much....I may think them through again...tomorrow."

"The things you would have done differently—I wonder—would you still have married young Abram of Ur?"

"Yes...only...sooner."

"Are you comfortable, Sarah?"

"Yes, but it is getting so...dark. Will you...light the lamp and put it...beside me here?

"That is much better. I want to look at my bracelet in the light. I have worn it every...day since you gave it to me."

"I know. It belongs to the matriarch of God's people, and it has in it the rich colors of Canaan."

"Yes, the blue sapphire is the...Sea of...Kinnereth and the....

"Abraham! The sapphire looks as though it is growing larger in the light! The...other stones...growing, too. Do you see them? How large...will they...get? I will hold my arm up high...so they will have more room to grow...and grow. Aren't they...beautiful?"

"Sarah, Sarah. The bracelet is the same as always."

"No! I can see long stretches of...each one of...these shining stones. They...go...so far...I can't see the end of them. They form bases of a city...a different kind of city than I have ever seen before. Never...dreamed of such a city as this one. I love all of Canaan, my husband, but you know I have also always liked cities too. This city would bedazzle...anyone...from Zoan to...Ur...and back ...again!

"Abraham? Can you hear me?"

"Yes, I hear. Can you tell me more about the city you see?"

"Yes, I want to tell you. It is...I am finding a word...be patient. It is...resplendent. Yes, that's it—resplendent!

"Abraham, for most of my...life...I have thought about a city that...would be our home place. I thought it...might have been founded at Moreh...so long ago. Then...thought...might be in...green valley between Mt. Ebal and Mt....Gerizim. I suppose I thought every place we stopped in those early years would be...place...of city ...we would build...call home.

"But now—do you see that city...in the distance? It is getting...plainer all the time. I am glad we did not stop anywhere else...not like any place in Canaan...or Egypt...Chaldees. See it? Jasper walls...so much gold. And each one of my stones, my Canaan-colored stones— stretched beyond belief...they are strong, glorious ...foundations of chalcedony, emerald, carnelian... topaz...

"Abraham, are you here with me?"

"Yes, Princess."

"Do you see the city?"

"Not yet, not as plainly as you do."

"How could...such a city...be?"

"Who do you think made it, Sarah?"

"Could only...be One?"

"What is His name?"

"He has many names...more than we...even know yet. But He is the one God...He is builder and maker...of this city. He is El Elyon. He is El Shaddai, El Olam.

"Abraham, it is good to be home..."

Sarah's Story has only just begun.

The Ancient World

Mediterranean Sea

Damascus

Sid

Tyre

Shec

Jerusalem

Je

Hebron

Beer-sheba

Memphis

EGYPT

SINAI

MIDIAN

Nile

Red Sea

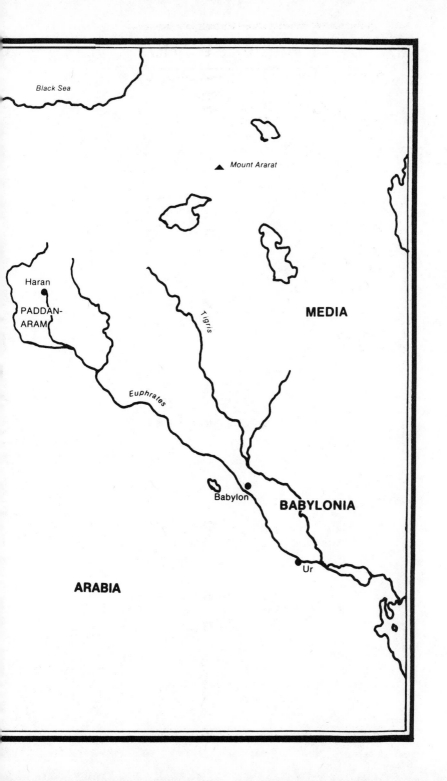